Edward S. Ellis

The Youth's Plutarch's Lives for Boys and Girls

Containing Brief and Accurate Accounts of the Lives of Famous Greeks and Romans

Edward S. Ellis

The Youth's Plutarch's Lives for Boys and Girls
Containing Brief and Accurate Accounts of the Lives of Famous Greeks and Romans

ISBN/EAN: 9783337041823

Printed in Europe, USA, Canada, Australia, Japan

Cover: Foto ©ninafisch / pixelio.de

More available books at **www.hansebooks.com**

THE YOUTH'S
PLUTARCH'S LIVES

FOR BOYS AND GIRLS

CONTAINING

BRIEF AND ACCURATE ACCOUNTS
OF THE LIVES OF FAMOUS
GREEKS AND ROMANS

EDITED

WITH INTRODUCTION AND NOTES BY

EDWARD S. ELLIS, M.A.

*Author of "The Young People's Standard History of the
United States;" "Common Errors in Writing and
Speaking;" "The Youth's Classical Diction-
ary;" "The Youth's Dictionary of
Mythology," etc.*

NEW YORK
THE WOOLFALL COMPANY
1895

COPYRIGHTED BY
THE WOOLFALL COMPANY
1895

CONTENTS.

	PAGE
INTRODUCTION,	5
THESEUS,	15
ROMULUS,	20
LYCURGUS,	24
NUMA,	31
SOLON,	36
PUBLICOLA,	40
THEMISTOCLES,	42
CAMILLUS,	45
PERICLES,	50
FABIUS MAXIMUS,	56
ALCIBIADES,	63
CAIUS MARCIUS CORIOLANUS,	67
TIMOLEON,	70
PAULUS ÆMILIUS,	73
PELOPIDAS,	77
MARCELLUS,	79
ARISTIDES,	84
CATO, THE CENSOR,	86
PHILOPŒMEN,	90
TITUS QUINCTIUS FLAMINIUS,	91
PYRRHUS,	93
CAIUS MARIUS,	98
LYSANDER,	102
SYLLA,	105

CONTENTS.

	PAGE
CIMON,	108
LUCULLUS,	109
NICIAS,	118
MARCUS CRASSUS,	123
SERTORIUS,	126
EUMENES,	130
AGESILAUS,	133
POMPEY,	135
ALEXANDER,	154
JULIUS CÆSAR,	171
PHOCION,	182
CATO, THE YOUNGER,	183
AGIS,	185
CLEOMENES,	188
TIBERIUS GRACCHUS,	192
CAIUS GRACCHUS,	194
DEMOSTHENES,	197
CICERO,	202
DEMETRIUS,	208
ANTONY,	211
DION,	215
MARCUS BRUTUS,	218
ARTAXERXES,	220
ARATUS,	222
WEIGHTS, MEASURES, AND MONEY,	224
CHRONOLOGICAL TABLE,	225
INDEX,	231

INTRODUCTION.

THE name of Plutarch will be remembered through all ages to come. He was born at Chæronea, in Bœotia, Greece, probably about A.D. 45 or 50, and studied philosophy under Ammonius at Delphi, at the time of Nero's visit to Greece, 66 A.D. Plutarch traveled extensively in Italy, visited Egypt, and spent some time in Rome, where he lectured on philosophy. Returning to his native city, he held office as a magistrate and died at an advanced age. He is known to have married, and was the father of at least five children, of whom two sons survived to manhood.

This famous scholar wrote many works, there being sixty extant bearing his name and treating of various subjects. They were collected under the common title of *Moralia* and translated into English by several authors. The work, however, which made him famous in antiquity, and afterward in all time, is his *Parallel Lives*, edited by C. Sintenis (4 volumes, Leipsic, 1639–53), and translated into all European languages. It has been translated into English several times by North, under the name of Dryden, and by John and William Langhorne. The Dryden translation was revised and corrected by A. H. Clough. It consists of forty-six biographies, divided into pairs—one from Greek and one from Roman history.

The question naturally occurs as to why this work has exercised such a charm over young and old, educated and uneducated, through the past centuries, and why such charm has in no way diminished to-day. There are two causes: the subjects treated and their method of treatment. The subjects are men who in their lives were the workers-out of the destiny of their time, and who after they crumbled to dust became models in all the after ages for those who aspire to become great and to make their impress upon human events. Plutarch attempts no analyses of the genius of those men and of their influence, but with a quick outline of the political and historical stature of the man, he vivifies his character by a series of personal traits which are as comprehensible to the uneducated as to the educated mind. While he is not a historian, he is always instructive and entertaining, for he himself possessed comprehensive knowledge, was sympathetic with all that was great and good, and wielded a pen that never failed to charm because it was tipped with the fire of genius.

Anything relating to this extraordinary genius is interesting. His wife was Timoxena, the daughter of Alexion. Late in life a daughter was born to them but died. How pathetic and lofty is the letter addressed to his wife upon learning of the death of this beloved child!

"Plutarch to his wife, greeting: The messengers you sent to announce our child's death apparently missed the road to Athens. I was told about my daughter on reaching Tanagra. Everything relating to the funeral I suppose to have been already performed;

my desire is that all these arrangements may have been so made as will now and in the future be most consoling to yourself. If there is anything which you have wished to do and have omitted, awaiting my opinion, and which you think would be a relief to you, it shall be attended to, apart from all excess and superstition, which no one would like less than yourself. Only, my wife, let me hope, that you will maintain both me and yourself within the reasonable limits of grief. What our loss really amounts to, I know and estimate for myself. But should I find your grief excessive, my trouble on your account will be greater than on that of our loss. I am not a 'stock or stone,' as you, my partner in the care of our numerous children, every one of whom we have ourselves brought up at home, can testify. And this child, a daughter, born to your wishes after four sons, and affording me the opportunity of recording your name, I am well aware was a special object of affection."

After referring to the sweet temper and loving ways of the child, the father says:

"Yet why should we forget the reasonings we have often addressed to others, and regard our present pain as obliterating and effacing our former joys?" The letter closes with expressions of his belief in the immortality of every human soul.

A great man it may be said is great in small things. Plutarch was as attentive to his humbler as to his more important duties. Referring to Epaminondas as giving dignity to the office of chief scavenger, he says: "And I, too, for that matter, am often a jest to my neighbors, when they see me, as they frequently do, in public, occupied on very similar duties; but the story told about Antisthenes comes to my assistance. When some one expressed surprise at his carrying home some pickled fish from market in his own hands. '*It is,*' he answered, '*for myself.*' Conversely, when I am reproached with standing by and watching while tiles are measured out, and stone and mortar brought up. *This service*, I say, *is not for myself*, it is for my country."

It should be borne in mind that Plutarch's

Lives are biography, not history. In the words of Montaigne, "He is a philosopher that teaches us virtue. It was probably his purpose to show that the great men of his native land had no cause to fear comparison with those of proud Rome, which led him to give the biographies in pairs, one Greek and one Roman in each pair, but such a great man as Plutarch could not be partial or morally undignified. He condemned and commended with unerring judgment, and sought to bring back to the Romans a reminder of the qualities which in their forefathers conquered the world, "and to indicate that oft-proven certainty that the loss of moral sanity must sooner or later entail political disintegration and national decay."

It is a singular fact that the *Lives* were translated and printed in Latin more than a century before the appearance of the first printed edition of the original Greek *works*. Amyot, a French abbé, published a translation in the reign of Henry II. of England, from which Sir T. North rendered it into English in the time of Queen Elizabeth. By careful research, Amyot made many corrections in the text. Dryden lent his name to a translation written by probably a score of different hands, with the inevitable result of "a motley work, full of errors, irregularities and inconsistencies." The appearance of the admirable translation by John and William Langhorne removed the necessity for any other.

We have deemed it advisable to place at the head of each biography a summary of its salient points. Plutarch gave little attention to dates, and while it is impossible to recall the words of his captivating narratives, it is easy to fix in the mind the important and leading facts in the career of those whose lives he relates. This will supply the historical data necessary to a complete understanding of the biography.

The eulogies of Plutarch are immeasurable. King Henry IV. of France, upon being told that his wife was pleased with the perusal of Plutarch's *Lives*, wrote to her: "You could not have sent me tidings more agreeable. To love Plutarch is to love me, for he was the instructor of my early years; and my good mother, to whom I owe so much, who watched over the formation of my character, and who was wont to say that she had no desire to see her son an illustrious ignoramus, put this book into my hands when I was little more than an infant at the breast. It has been my conscience, and has whispered in my ear many good suggestions and maxims for my conduct and the government of my affairs."

Jean Jacques Rousseau affirmed that he never read Plutarch without profit; Madame Roland referred to it as "the pasture of great souls," and Ralph Waldo Emerson made the prophecy that "Plutarch will be perpetually re-discovered from time to time, as long as books last."

It is to be deplored that many of the writings of this incomparable genius have disappeared beyond recovery. "What a triology is lost to mankind in his Lives of Scipio, Epaminondas, and Pindar!" Not a scrap remains of his commentaries on Homer and Hesiod, nor of his essays and fables.

The learned Theodorus Gaza, of the Fifteenth Century, uttered what is perhaps the most striking tribute ever rendered to the genius of Plutarch. Being asked that if learning were doomed to suffer general shipwreck, and it was given him to choose the one author that should survive, he replied, "Give me Plutarch."

Agathias, who flourished in the Sixth Century, is the author of the following epigram:

> "Chæronean Plutarch, to thy deathless praise
> Does martial Rome this grateful statue raise,
> Because both Greece and she thy fame have shared,
> (Their heroes written, and their lives compared).
> But thou thyself couldst never write thy own;
> Their lives have parallels, but thine has none."

E. S. E.

July, 1895.

THE YOUTH'S
PLUTARCH'S LIVES

OF

FAMOUS GREEKS AND ROMANS.

THESEUS.

Note.—THESEUS (Greek). About all that is known, in addition to the sketch given by Plutarch, of this famous king is that the facts occurred during the thirteenth century B.C.

THE mother of Theseus was Æthra, and in his youth he was committed to the care of Pittheus, his grandfather, governor of the small city of the Trœzenians. This man was reputed to be the possessor of wonderful knowledge and wisdom.

In his youth, Theseus displayed great strength of body, undaunted courage, and quickness alike of force and understanding. On the road to Athens, he slew Periphates, near Epidaurus, and took away his club; killed Sinnis, often surnamed the Bender of Pines; the Crommyonian Sow, called Phœa; and Sciron, said to have been a notorious robber (though others claim he was a good man). There were many victims to the prowess of Theseus, who, despite his numerous valiant exploits, was guilty of flagrant crimes and immoralities.

When Theseus arrived at manhood, he went to Delphi, as was the custom, to offer the first fruits of his hair to Apollo. He shaved, however, only the front part, as Homer tells us the Abantes did. Because of this, that kind of tonsure was called Theseis. The Abantes were a warlike people, who found that long hair was a disadvantage in close fighting, of which they were fond. It was for a similar reason that Alexander of Macedon ordered his troops to cut off their beards.

Theseus was a relative of the great Hercules, whose marvelous exploits fired him to imitation. After the deeds that have been referred to, Theseus, hoping to make himself popular with the Athenians, left Athens to fight with the bull of Marathon, which had done much mischief to the inhabitants of Tetrapolis. He captured the bull and brought him alive to Athens, where he was sacrificed to the Delphinian Apollo.

The next exploit of Theseus was against the Minotaur—

> "A mingled form, prodigious to behold,
> Half bull, half man."

Ariadne, daughter of the King of Crete, had fallen in love with Theseus, and gave him great help in this famous encounter, by handing to him a sword and a long thread. The latter was unwound, as he followed the devious turnings of the labyrinth to where the Minotaur sheltered himself, and gave the necessary guidance to Theseus in making his way out again. He slew the Minotaur, and carried away Ariadne with him.

On his return from Crete, Theseus put in at Delos; and having sacrificed to Apollo, and dedicated a statue to Venus, which he received from Ariadne, he joined the young men in a dance, which imitated the mazes and outlets of the labyrinth, in which the Minotaur had sheltered himself, and with all its varying movements performed in regular time. He also instituted games in Delos, where he originated the custom of giving a palm to the victors.

Drawing near Attica, Theseus and the pilot were in such high spirits that they forgot to hoist the sail which was to be the signal to Ægeus of their safety. He was so overcome with despair at their supposed death that he threw himself from the rock and was dashed to pieces.

Ægeus being dead, Theseus undertook a stupendous work. He sent to consult the oracle of Delphi concerning the fortune of his new government and city, and received this answer:

> "Son of the Pitthean maid,
> To your town the terms and fates
> My father gives of many states.
> Be not anxious nor afraid;
> The bladder will not fail to swim
> On the waves that compass him."

This was B.C. 1235. Theseus settled all the inhabitants of Attica in Athens, and made them one people in one city. He dissolved the corporations, councils, and courts of each particular town, and built one common Prytaneum and court hall. He resigned his kingly power, and organized the commonwealth under the auspices of the gods. He divided the people into noblemen, husbandmen, and mechanics. To the nobility were assigned the care of religion, the supplying of the city with magistrates, the expounding of the laws, and the interpretation of whatever related to the worship of the gods.

The nobles excelled in dignity, the husbandmen in usefulness, and the artificers in number. The money was stamped with the image of an ox, whence came the expression of a thing being worth ten or a hundred oxen.

Having conquered and annexed the country adjoining Megara, Theseus set up the famed pillar in the isthmus, and inscribed it with two verses to distinguish the boundaries. That on the east side ran:

"This is not Peloponnesus, but Ionia;"

and that on the west side was:

"This is Peloponnesus, not Ionia."

Theseus instituted games in imitation of Hercules, desirous that as the Greeks, in pursuance of that hero's appointment, celebrated the Olympic games in honor of Jupiter, so they should celebrate the Isthmian in honor of Neptune. He next made war with the Amazons, and received their queen Antiope, as the reward of his valor.

There are many contradictions in the various accounts of Theseus. Herodotus thinks that among all the famous expeditions of those times, the only one in which this hero was engaged was in assisting the Lapithæ against the Centaurs. Others claim that he attended Jason to Colchos, and Meleager in killing the boar, from which came the proverb—"Nothing without Theseus." It is admitted that he performed many amazing exploits, which gave rise to the saying, "This man is another Hercules."

Theseus aided Adrastus in recovering the bodies of those that fell before Thebes, by persuading the Thebans to a truce. Philochorus thinks this was the first truce ever known for burying the dead, though Hercules previous to this gave leave to his enemies to carry off their slain.

Incited by Menestheus, the Athenians rose against Theseus, and while he was occupied in suppressing the sedition, the Tyndaridæ declared war against him. Though Athens was thus placed in great danger, Menestheus persuaded the people to admit the Tyndaridæ and to treat them hospitably, since they were warring against Theseus alone.

Theseus was compelled to flee the country, and he applied for help to Lycomedes, king of the Scyrians. This monarch, either jealous of Theseus or anxious to oblige Menestheus, having led the hero to the highest cliffs of the country, on pretence of showing him his lands, threw him headlong from the rocks and killed him. An equally probable account is that Theseus slipped, while taking a walk, according to his custom, after supper. His death was disregarded, and Menestheus quietly possessed the kingdom of Athens, while the sons of Theseus attended Elephenor as private persons to the Trojan war.

After the Median war, Phædo being archon of Athens, the Athenians, consulting the oracle of Delphi, were commanded to gather together the bones of Theseus, and laying them in some honorable place, keep them as sacred in the city. It was hard to find the remains, because of the savage temper of the people who inhabited the island. When, however, it was conquered by Cimon, he chanced to see an eagle pecking with his beak, and tearing up the earth with his talons. As if by inspiration, he knew this was the burial-place of Theseus. Digging there, he found the coffin of a man of more than ordinary size, with a brazen spear-head and a sword lying by it. All these were taken on board Cimon's galley and brought to Athens, where they were interred with great honor.

ROMULUS.

Note.—ROMULUS (Roman). Romulus is considered to be the mythical founder of "imperial Rome," whose foundation was laid B.C. 753.

ROMULUS was the traditional founder of Rome; but from whom and for what cause the city obtained that name, historians are not agreed. The story goes that Romulus and his twin-brother

Remus were in their infancy thrown into the river Tiber, but were miraculously floated ashore and suckled by a she-wolf till they were found by a shepherd named Faustulus, who brought them up. The beauty and dignity of their persons, even in their childhood, promised a generous disposition, and as they grew up they both showed great courage and bravery. Grown to the state of manhood, they determined to build themselves a city; but while they were intent upon building, a dispute soon arose about the place. Romulus having built a square, which he called Rome, would have the city there; but Remus marked out a more secure situation on Mount Aventine, which, from him, was called Remonium. The dispute was referred to the decision of augury, the result being that Remus was highly incensed, and as Romulus was opening a ditch round the place where the walls were to be built, he ridiculed some parts of the work and obstructed others. At last, as he presumed to leap over it, some say he fell by the hands of Romulus, others by that of Celer, one of his companions. The day on which they began to build the city is allowed to be the 21st of April, B.C. 750.

When the city was built Romulus divided the younger part of the inhabitants into battalions. Each corps consisted of three thousand foot and three hundred horse, and was called a Legion; the rest of the multitude he called The People. A hundred of the most considerable citizens he took for his council, with the title of Patricians, and the whole body was called the Senate. To obtain wives for his citizens he planned a capture of Sabine women as follows:—He appointed by proclamation a day for a splendid sacrifice, with public games and shows. Multitudes assembled, and Romulus himself presided. At a pre-arranged signal the Romans rushed in with their swords drawn, and seized the daughters of the Sabines, but quietly suffered the men to escape. The Sabines demanded their women back, but were refused, whereupon Acron declared war with Romulus; but in single combat with Romulus he was killed, his army routed, and his city taken. On this occasion Romulus made a vow that if he conquered his enemy he would himself dedicate his adversary's arms to Jupiter.

Romulus having considered how he should perform his vow in the most acceptable manner to Jupiter, and withal make the procession most agreeable to his people, cut down a great oak that grew in the camp, and hewed it into the figure of a trophy; to this he fastened Acron's whole suit of armor, disposed in its proper form. Then he put on his own robes, and wearing a laurel crown on his head, his hair gracefully flowing, he took the trophy erect upon his right shoulder, and so marched on, singing the song of victory before his troops, who followed completely armed, while the citizens received him with joy and admiration. This procession was the origin and model of future triumphs.

In a subsequent battle with the Sabines, while

the conflict was at its height the ardor of the combatants was repressed by an astonishing spectacle. The daughters of the Sabines, that had been forcibly carried off, rushed with loud cries and lamentations, like persons distracted, amidst the drawn swords, and over the dead bodies, to come at their husbands and fathers, some carrying their infants in their arms, some darting forward with dishevelled hair, but all calling by turns both upon the Sabines and Romans by the tenderest names. Both parties were extremely moved, and room was made for them between the two armies. Their lamentations pierced to the utmost ranks, and all were deeply affected, particularly when their upbraiding and complaints ended in supplication and entreaty.

After much negotiation peace was concluded, and the Sabines were incorporated with the Romans. Many honorable privileges, however, were conferred upon the women, some of which were these: That the men should give them the way wherever they met them; that they should not mention an obscene word, nor act indecently before them; that in case of their killing any person, they should not be tried before the ordinary judges; and that their children should wear an ornament about their necks, called Bulla, from its likeness to a bubble, and a garment bordered with purple.

After the wars Romulus behaved as almost all men do who rise by some great and unexpected good fortune to dignity and power; for, exalted with his exploits, and loftier in his sentiments, he dropped his popular affability, and assumed the monarch to an odious degree. He gave the first offence by his dress; his habit being a purple vest, over which he wore a robe bordered with purple. He gave audience in a chair of state. He had always about him a number of young men called Celeres, from their dispatch in doing business; and before him went men with staves, called lictors, to keep off the populace, who also wore thongs of leather at their girdles, ready to bind directly any person he should order to be bound.

Romulus disappeared in an unaccountable manner at the age of fifty-four, in the thirty-eighth year of his reign.

LYCURGUS.

Note.—LYCURGUS (Spartan). This celebrated Spartan legislator, whose existence is doubted by some modern critics, is said to have lived in the ninth century B.C.

OF Lycurgus, the lawgiver, we have nothing to relate that is certain and uncontroverted. For there are different accounts of his birth, his travels, his death, and especially of the laws and form of government which he established. But least of all are the times agreed upon in which this great man lived. After reigning over the Spartans eight months he set sail for Crete, and while there he was struck with admiration of some of the Cretan laws, and he resolved at his return to make use of them in Sparta. From Crete Lycurgus passed to Asia, desirous, as is said, to compare the Ionian expense and luxury with the Cretan frugality and hard diet, so as to judge what effect each had on their several manners and governments. There also, probably, he met with Homer's poems, which were preserved by the posterity of Cleophylus. Observing that many moral sentences and much political knowledge were intermixed with his stories, which had an irresistible charm, he collected them into one body, and transcribed them with pleasure, in order to take them home with him. For his glorious poetry was not yet fully known in Greece; only some particular pieces were in a few hands, as they happen to be dispersed. Lycurgus was the first that made them generally known.

Among the many new institutions of Lycurgus the first and most important was that of a senate; which sharing, as Plato says, in the power of the kings, too imperious and unrestrained before, and having equal authority with them, was the means of keeping them within the bounds of moderation, and highly contributed to the preservation of the State; for before it had been veering and unsettled, sometimes inclining to arbitrary power, and sometimes toward a pure democracy; but this establishment of a senate, an intermediate body, like ballast, kept it in a just equilibrium, and put it in a safe posture.

A second and bolder political enterprise of Lycurgus was a division of the land. He made nine thousand lots for the territory of Sparta, which he distributed among so many citizens, and thirty thousand for the inhabitants of the rest of Laconia. Each lot was capable of producing, one year with another, seventy bushels of grain for each man, and twelve for each woman, besides a quantity of wine and oil in proportion. Such a provision they thought sufficient for health and a good habit of body, and they wanted nothing more.

After this he attempted to divide also the movables, in order to take away all appearance of inequality; but he soon perceived that they could not bear to have their goods directly taken from them, and therefore took another method, counterworking their avarice by a stratagem. First, he stopped the currency of the gold and silver coin, and ordered that they should make use of iron money only; then to a great quantity and weight of this he assigned but a very small value; so that to lay up ten minæ a whole room was required, and to remove it nothing less than a yoke of oxen. When this became current many kinds of injustice ceased in Lacedæmon. Who would steal or take a bribe, who would defraud or rob, when he could not conceal the booty, when he could neither be dignified by the possession of it, nor, if cut in pieces, be served by its use?

Desirous to complete the conquest of luxury and to exterminate the love of riches, he introduced a third institution, which was wisely enough and ingeniously contrived. This was the use of public tables, where all were to eat in common of the same meat, and such kinds of it as were appointed by law.

The rich were more offended with this regulation than with any other, and rising in a body they loudly expressed their indignation; nay, they proceeded so far as to assault Lycurgus with stones, and in the disturbance he had one of his eyes knocked out. Children also were introduced at these public tables, as so many schools of sobriety. There they heard discourses concerning government, and were instructed in the most liberal breeding. There they were allowed to jest without scurrility, and were not to take it ill when the raillery was returned. For it was reckoned worthy of a Lacedæmonian to bear a jest; but if any one's patience failed, he had only to desire them to be quiet, and they left off immediately. When they first entered, the oldest man present pointed to the door, and said—"Not a word spoken in this company goes out there."

A third ordinance of Lycurgus was, that they should not often make war against the same enemy, lest, by being frequently put upon defending themselves, they too should become able warriors in their turn.

As for the education of youth, which he looked upon as the greatest and most glorious work of a lawgiver, he began with it at the very source. He ordered the virgins to exercise themselves in running, wrestling, and throwing quoits and darts; that their bodies being strong and vigorous, their children might be the same.

It was not left to the father to rear what children he pleased, but he was obliged to carry the child to a place called Lesche, to be examined by the most ancient men of the tribe, who were assembled there. If it was strong and well proportioned, they gave orders for its education, and assigned it one of the nine thousand shares of land; but if it was weakly and deformed, they ordered it to be thrown into the place called Apothetæ, which is a deep cavern near the mountain Taygetus, concluding that its life could be no advantage either to itself or to the public, since Nature had not given it at first any strength or goodness of constitution. For the same reason, the women did not wash their new-born infants with water, but with wine, thus making some trial of their habit of body; imagining that sickly and epileptic children sink and die under the experiment, while the healthy become more vigorous and hardy.

As for learning, they had just what was absolutely necessary. They wrote to be read, and spoke to be understood. They were very spare in their diet, so that they might grow tall. For when the animal spirits are not too much oppressed by a great quantity of food, which stretches itself out in breadth and thickness, they mount upwards by their natural lightness, and the body easily and freely shoots up in height. This also contributes to make them handsome; for thin and slender habits yield more freely to Nature, which then gives a fine proportion to the limbs; whilst the heavy and gross resist her by their weight.

Lycurgus was short and sententious in his discourse, if we may judge by some of his answers which are recorded; that, for instance, concerning the constitution. When one advised him to establish a popular government in Lacedæmon, —"Go," said he, "and first make a trial of it in thy own family." That again, concerning sacrifices to the deity, when he was asked why he appointed them so trifling, and of so little value?— "That we may never be in want," said he, "of something to offer him." The Spartans hated long speeches. Even when they indulged a vein of pleasantry, one might perceive that they would not use one unnecessary word, nor let an expression escape them that had not some sense worth attending to. For one being asked to go and hear a person who imitated the nightingale to perfection, answered—"I have heard the nightingale herself." Nor were poetry and music less cultivated among them than a concise dignity of expression. Their songs had a spirit which could rouse the soul, and impel it in an enthusiastic manner to action. The language was plain and manly, the subject serious and moral. At the public games they relaxed the severity of their discipline, the men dressing their hair in curious fashions. They let their hair grow from their youth, but took more particular care, when they expected an action, to have it well combed and shining, remembering a saying of Lycurgus, that "a large head of hair made the handsome more graceful and the ugly more terrible."

Lawsuits were banished from Lacedæmon with money. The Spartans knew neither riches nor poverty, but possessed an equal competency, and had a cheap and easy way of supplying their few wants.

Their discourse seldom turned upon money or business or trade, but upon the praise of the excellent or the contempt of the worthless; and the last was expressed with that pleasantry and humor which conveyed instruction and correction without seeming to intend it. Nor was Lycurgus himself immoderately severe in his manner; for he dedicated a little statue to the god of laughter in each hall. He considered facetiousness as a seasoning of their hard exercise and diet, and therefore ordered it to take place on all proper occasions, in their common entertainments and parties of pleasure. Upon the whole, he taught his citizens to think nothing more disagreeable than to live by (or for) themselves. Like bees, they acted with one impulse for the general good, and always assembled about their prince. They were possessed with a thirst of honor, an enthusiasm bordering upon insanity, and had not a wish but for their country.

Lycurgus likewise made good regulations with respect to burials. In the first place, to take away all superstition, he ordered the dead to be buried in the city, and even permitted their monuments to be erected near the temples; accustoming the youth to such sights from their infancy, that they might have no uneasiness from them, nor any horror for death, as if people were polluted with the touch of a dead body, or with treading upon a grave. In the next place, he suffered nothing to be buried with the corpse except the red cloth and the olive leaves in which it was wrapped. Nor would he suffer the relations to inscribe any names upon the tombs, except of those men that fell in battle, or those women who died in some sacred office. He fixed eleven days for the time of mourning; on the twelfth they were to put an end to it, after offering sacrifice to Ceres. No part of life was left vacant and unimproved; but even with their necessary actions he interwove the praise of virtue and the contempt of vice; and he so filled the city with living examples that it was next to impossible for persons who had these from their infancy before their eyes not to be drawn and formed to honor. Lycurgus is reported to have starved himself to death.

NUMA.

Note.—NUMA (Roman). Numa Pompilius was the second mythical king of Rome, and, according to legend, was elected after the death of Romulus. He flourished in the eighth century B.C., and reigned some forty years. About B.C. 180, a pretended discovery was made of the sacred books of Numa.

NUMA was born at Cures, a city of the Sabines, from which the Romans, together with the incorporated Sabines, took the name of Quirites. He was the son of a person of distinction, named Pomponius. It seemed to be by the direction of the gods that he was born on the 21st of April, the same day that Rome was founded by Romulus. His mind was naturally disposed to virtue; and he still further subdued it by discipline, patience, and philosophy; not only purging it of the grosser passions, but even of that ambition and rapaciousness which was reckoned honorable amongst the barbarians—persuaded that true fortitude consists in the conquest of appetites by reason. On this account he banished all luxury and splendor from his house; and both citizens and strangers found him a faithful counselor and an upright judge. As for his hours of leisure, he spent them not in the pursuits of pleasure, or schemes of profit, but in the worship of the gods, and in rational inquiries into their nature and their power.

At the age of forty Numa, on the death of Romulus, was elected king; but he declined the crown until he was persuaded by his father and Marcius to accept it. His first act of government was to discharge the body of three hundred men called Celeres, whom Romulus always kept about him as guards, for he neither chose to distrust those who put confidence in him, nor to reign over a people that could distrust him. To him is attributed the institution of that high order of priests called Pontifices, over which he is said to have presided himself. The Pontifex Maximus, or chief priest, had care not only of public sacrifices, but even of private rites and offerings. To Numa also is ascribed the establishment of the Vestal Virgins and the whole sacrifice with respect to the perpetual fire which they watch continually. If this light happens by accident to be put out, as the sacred lamp is said to have been at Athens under the tyranny of Ariston, at Delphi when the temple was burned by the Medes, and at Rome in the Mithridatic war, as also in the civil war (when not only was the fire extinguished but the altar overturned),—the lamp is not lighted again from another fire, but new fire is gained by drawing a pure unpolluted flame from the sunbeams. They generally kindled it with concave vessels of brass formed by the conic section of a right-angled triangle, whose lines from the circumference meet in one central point. This being placed against the sun causes the rays to converge in the center, which, by reflection, acquiring the force and activity of fire, rarefy the air, and immediately kindle such light and dry matter as they think fit to apply.

Numa taught the Pontifices to look upon the last offices to the dead as no pollution. He likewise fixed the time of mourning according to the different ages of the deceased. He allowed none for a child that died under three years of age; and for one older the mourning was only to last as many months as he lived years, provided those were not more than ten. The longest mourning was not to continue above ten months, after which space widows were permitted to marry again.

No occupation implants so speedy and so effectual a love of peace as a country life; where there remains indeed courage and bravery sufficient to defend the property, the temptations to injustice and avarice are removed. Numa, therefore, introduced among his subjects an attachment to husbandry as a charm of peace, and contriving a business for them which would rather form their manners to simplicity than raise them to opulence. He divided the country into several portions, which he called pagi or boroughs, and appointed over each of them a governor or overseer. Sometimes also he inspected them himself; and, judging of the disposition of the people by the condition of their farms, some he advanced to posts of honor and trust; and, on the other hand, he reprimanded and endeavored to reform the negligent and the idle. But the most admired of all his institutions is his distribution of the citizens into companies.

This distribution was made according to the several arts or trades, of musicians, goldsmiths, masons, dyers, shoemakers, tanners, braziers, and potters. He collected the other artificers also into companies, who had their respective halls, courts, and religious ceremonies, peculiar to each society. By these means he first took away the distinction of Sabines and Romans, subjects of Tatius and subjects of Romulus, both name and thing; the very separation into parts mixing and incorporating the whole together.

He attempted the reformation of the calendar

too, which he executed with some degree of skill, though not with absolute exactness. In the reign of Romulus it had neither measure nor order, some months consisting of fewer than twenty days, while some were stretched to thirty-five, and others even to more. They had no idea of the difference between the annual course of the sun and that of the moon, and only laid down the proposition that the year consisted of 360 days. Numa, then, observing that there was a difference of eleven days, 354 days making up the lunar year and 365 the solar, doubled those eleven days, and inserted them as an intercalary month after that of February every other year. He likewise altered the order of the months, making March third, which was first, and January and February first and second, which in the time of Romulus were eleventh and twelfth. Many, however, assert that the two months of January and February were added by Numa, whereas before they had reckoned but ten months in the year. Of this we have a proof in the name of the last, for it is still called December or the tenth month; and that March was the first is also evident, because the fifth from it was called Quintilis, the sixth Sextilis, and so the rest in their order. If January and February had then been placed before March, the month Quintilis would have been the fifth in name, but the seventh in reckoning. Besides, it is reasonable to conclude that the month of March, dedicated by Romulus to the god Mars, should stand first. Numa seems to have taken away the precedency from March, which is denominated from the god of war, with a design to show his preference of the political to the martial virtues. For Janus, in the most remote antiquity, being remarkable for his political abilities and his cultivation of society, reclaimed men from their rude and savage manners. He is therefore represented with two faces, as having altered the former state of the world, and given quite a new turn to life. He had also a temple at Rome with two gates, which it was customary to open in the time of war and to shut in time of peace. The latter was seldom the case till Numa's reign, when, however, it was not opened for one day, but stood constantly shut during the space of forty-three years.

Numa wasted away insensibly with old age and a gentle decline, and was some few years above eighty when he died.

SOLON.

Note.—SOLON (Greek). Solon, one of the seven sages of Greece, was born at Salamis in the seventh century B.C. He was chosen archon, B.C. 594, and is supposed to have died at the age of 80, about B.C. 558.

SOLON was a celebrated Grecian lawyer. His father, Execestides, having hurt his fortune by indulging his great and munificent spirit in assisting others, was ashamed himself to accept assistance, and Solon had to apply himself to merchandise. Some, however, say that he traveled rather to gratify his curiosity and extend his knowledge than to raise an estate. For he professed his love of wisdom, and, when far advanced in years, made this declaration,—"I grow in learning as I grow in years." That he was not too much attached to wealth we may gather from the following lines:—

> " The man that boasts of golden stores,
> Of grain that loads his bending floors,
> Of fields with fresh'ning herbage green,
> Where bounding steeds and herds are seen,
> I call not happier than the swain,
> Whose limbs are sound, whose food is plain,
> Whose joys a blooming wife endears,
> Whose hours a smiling offspring cheers."

The profession of merchandise was honorable, as it brought home the produce of barbarous countries, engaged the friendship of kings, and opened a wide field of knowledge and experience. Nay, some merchants have been founders of great cities; Protus, for instance, who built Marseilles. Thales also, and Hippocrates, the mathematician, are said to have had their share in commerce; and the oil that Plato disposed of in Egypt defrayed the expense of his travels.

It was a saying of Solon that "absolute monarchy is a fair field, but it has no outlet."

The first of his public acts was that debts should be forgiven, and that no man for the future should take the body of his debtor for security; and some friends of his who knew of his intention, taking advantage of the secret before the decree took place, borrowed large sums of the rich and purchased estates with them. Afterwards, when the decree was published, they kept their possessions, without paying the money they had taken up; which brought great reflections upon Solon, as if he had not been imposed upon with the rest, but were rather an accomplice in the fraud. This charge, however, was soon removed by his being the first to comply with the law, and remitting a debt which he had out at interest. But his friends went by the name of Chreocopidæ, or debt-cutters, ever after.

He repealed the laws of Draco, except those concerning murder, because of the severity of the punishments they appointed, which for almost all offenses were capital. Even those that were convicted of idleness were to suffer death, and such as stole only a few apples or pot-herbs were to be punished in the same manner as sacrilegious persons and murderers. Hence the saying that "Draco wrote his laws, not with ink but with blood."

He established the council of the Areopagus, which was to consist of such as had borne the office of archon, and himself was one of the number. But observing that the people, now discharged from their debts, grew insolent and imperious, he proceeded to constitute another council or senate of four hundred, a hundred out of each tribe, by whom all affairs were to be previously considered; and ordered that, without their approbation, no matter should be laid before the general assembly. In the mean time, the high court of the Areopagus were to be the inspectors and guardians of the laws.

Solon's law is justly commended which forbids men to speak ill of the dead. His law concerning wills has likewise its merit, for he gave every man the full and free disposal of his own.

He regulated, moreover, the journeys of women, their mournings and sacrifices, and endeavored to keep them clear of all disorder and excess. They were not to go out of town with more than three habits; the provisions they carried with them were not to exceed the value of an obolus; their basket was not to be above a cubit high; and in the night they were not to travel but in a carriage, with a torch before them. At funerals they were forbidden to tear themselves, and no hired mourner was to utter lamentable notes, or to act in any way that tended to excite sorrow. He made a law that no son should be obliged to maintain his father if he had not taught him a trade. His regulations with respect to the planting of trees were also very judicious. He that planted any tree in his field was to place it at least five feet from his neighbor's ground; and if it was a fig-tree or an olive, nine; for these extend their roots further than others, and their neighborhood is prejudicial to some trees, not only as they take away the nourishment, but as their effluvia is noxious. He that would dig a pit or a ditch was to dig it as far from another man's ground as it was deep; and if any one would raise stocks of bees, he was to place them three hundred feet from those already raised by another.

These are some of the most noticeable of the laws of Solon. He made the Athenians take an oath to observe his laws for 100 years, but after an absence of ten years in Egypt he found his laws disregarded, and he retired to Cyprus, where he helped to build a city called Soli, and died at the age of 80 years.

PUBLICOLA.

Note.—PUBLICOLA (Roman). Valerius Publicola was one of the founders of the Roman republic, and flourished in the sixth century B.C.

PUBLICOLA was so called by the Romans in acknowledgment of his merit. He was a son of Valerius, and was descended from that ancient Valerius who was the principal author of the union between the Romans and the Sabines. Our Valerius distinguished himself by his eloquence and riches even while Rome was yet under kingly government. His eloquence he employed with great propriety and spirit in defense of justice, and his riches in relieving the necessitous. Hence it was natural to conclude that if the government should become republican, his station in it would soon be one of the most eminent.

The famous eulogium which he pronounced over the body of Brutus* gave rise to the custom

* Lucius Junius Brutus (*not* Marcus Brutus).

of funeral orations. The Romans were so much charmed with the speech that afterward all the great and illustrious men amongst them, upon their decease, had their encomium from persons of distinction. This funeral oration was more ancient than any amongst the Greeks, unless we allow that Anaximenes, the orator, relates that Solon was the author of this custom.

Desirous to make his high office, as well as himself, rather agreeable than formidable to the people, he ordered the axes to be taken away from the rods, and that, whenever he went to the great assembly, the rods should be lowered in respect to the citizens, as if the supreme power were lodged in them; a custom which the consuls observe to this day. The people were not aware that by this he did not lessen his own power (as they imagined), but only by such an instance of moderation obviated and cut off all occasion of envy, and gained as much authority to his person as he seemed to take from his office; for they all submitted to him with pleasure, and were so much charmed with his behavior that they gave him the name of Publicola, that is, the people's respectful friend. He not only acquired but employed his riches honorably, for he was a generous benefactor to the poor; so that if Solon was the wisest, Publicola was the happiest of humankind.

THEMISTOCLES.

Note.—THEMISTOCLES (Greek). This statesman and general was born in the latter half of the sixth century B.C. His death (attributed by Plutarch to suicide by poison, though the account is doubted), occurred at Magnesia, Asia Minor, B.C. 470 or 472.

THEMISTOCLES was an Athenian general. He had an early and violent inclination for public business, and was so strongly smitten with the love of glory, with an ambition of the highest station, that he involved himself in troublesome quarrels with persons of the first rank and influence in the State, particularly with Aristides, the son of Lysimachus, who always opposed him.

When Themistocles went to the Olympic games he endeavored to equal or exceed Cimon in the elegance of his table, the splendor of his pavilions, and other expenses of his train. These things, however, were not agreeable to the Greeks; they looked upon them as suitable to a young man of a noble family; but when an obscure person set himself up so much above his fortune, he gained nothing by it but the imputation of vanity.

At length, having attained to a great height of power and popularity, his faction prevailed, and he procured the banishment of Aristides by what is called the Ostracism.

Though the several engagements with the Persian fleet in the straits of Eubœa were not decisive, yet they were of great advantage to the Greeks, who learned, by experience, that neither the number of ships, nor the beauty and splendor of their ornaments, nor the vaunting shouts and songs of the barbarians, have anything dreadful in them to men that know how to fight hand to hand, and are determined to behave gallantly. These things they were taught to despise, when they came to close action, and grappled with the foe. In this case Pindar's sentiments appear just, when he says of the fight at Artemisium,—

> "'Twas then that Athens the foundation laid
> Of Liberty's fair structure."

Indeed, intrepid courage is the commencement of victory.

At the battle of Salamis, against Xerxes, King of Persia, Themistocles had charge of the fleet. He was happy in choosing a place for action, and no less so in taking advantage of a proper time for it. He would not engage the enemy till that time of day when a brisk wind usually rises from the sea, which occasions a high surf in the channel. This was no inconvenience to the Grecian vessels, which were low built and well compacted; but a very great one to the Persian ships, which had high sterns and lofty decks, and were heavy and unwieldy; for it caused them to veer in such a manner that their sides were exposed to the Greeks, who attacked them furiously. During the whole engagement great attention was given to the motions of Themistocles. Ariamenes, the

Persian admiral, a man of distinguished honor, and by far the bravest of the king's brothers, directed his maneuvers chiefly against him. His ship was very tall, and from thence he threw darts, and shot forth arrows as from the walls of a castle. But Aminias the Decelean, and Sosicles the Pedian, who were both in one ship, bore down upon him with their prow, and both ships meeting they were fastened together by means of their brazen beaks; when Ariamenes boarding their galley, they received him with their pikes, and pushed him into the sea. The first man that took a ship was an Athenian named Lycomedes, captain of a galley, who cut down the ensigns from the enemy's ship, and consecrated them to the laureled Apollo. As the Persians could come up in the straits but few at a time, and often put each other in confusion, the Greeks equaling them in the line, fought them till the evening, when they broke them entirely, and gained that signal and complete victory, than which no other naval achievement, either of the Greeks or barbarians, ever was more glorious.

Having returned from the wars, his next enterprise was to rebuild and fortify Athens. After this he built and fortified the Piræus (having observed the great convenience of that harbor) by which means he gave the city every maritime accommodation. In this respect his politics were very different from those of the ancient kings of Athens, who endeavored to draw the attention of their subjects from the business of navigation, so that they might turn it entirely to the culture of the ground.

Having given offense to the people, he was banished by the Ostracism; but this was nothing more than they had done to others whose power was become a burden to them, and who had risen above the quality which a commonwealth requires; for the Ostracism, or ten years' banishment, was not so much intended to punish this or that great man, as to pacify and mitigate the fury of envy, that delights in the disgrace of superior characters, and loses a part of its rancor by their fall.

On the revolt of Egypt he was asked to take the direction of an expedition, but he declined, and soon afterwards destroyed himself, it is said, by drinking bull's blood. He was sixty-six years old when he died. Plato, the comedian (not the philosopher), says of him,

> "Oft as the merchant speeds the passing sail,
> Thy tomb, Themistocles, he stops to hail;
> When hostile ships in martial combat meet,
> Thy shade, attending, hovers o'er the fleet."

CAMILLUS.

Note.—CAMILLUS (Roman). Camillus Marcus Furius, lived in the fourth century B.C. Much that is related of him is fabulous. His son raised a rebellion in Dalmatia, during the reign of Claudius, but was abandoned by his soldiers and committed suicide.

AMONG the many remarkable things related of Furius Camillus, the most extraordinary seems to be this, that though he was often in the highest commands, and performed the greatest actions, though he was six times chosen dictator, though he triumphed four times, and was styled the second founder of Rome, yet he was never once consul. This was, however, because in his time military tribunes were appointed instead of consuls. There is upon record a very laudable act of his, that took place during his office. As the wars had made many widows, he obliged such of the men as lived single, partly by persuasion, and partly by threatening them with fines, to marry those widows. One of his most important exploits was the siege of Veii. Perceiving that it would be both difficult and dangerous to endeavor to take the city by assault, he ordered mines to be dug, the soil about it being easy to work, and admitting of depth enough for the works to be carried on unseen by the enemy. As this succeeded to his wish, he made an assault without to call the enemy to the walls; and in the mean time others of his soldiers made their way through the mines and secretly penetrated to Juno's temple in the citadel.

The city thus taken by the Romans sword in hand, while they were busy in plundering it and carrying off its immense riches, Camillus beholding from the citadel what was done, at first burst into tears; and when those about him began to magnify his happiness at his success, he lifted up his hands toward heaven and uttered this prayer: —"Great Jupiter, and ye gods, that have the inspection of our good and evil actions, ye know that the Romans, not without just cause, but in their own defense, and constrained by necessity, have made war against this city, and its unjust inhabitants. If we must have some misfortune in lieu of this success, I entreat that it may fall not upon Rome, or the Roman army, but upon myself; yet lay not, ye gods, a heavy hand upon me!"

Whether it was that Camillus was elated with his great exploit in taking a city that was the rival of Rome, after it had been besieged ten years, or that he was misled by his flatterers, he took upon him too much state for a magistrate subject to the laws and usages of his country. For his triumph was conducted with excessive pomp, and he rode through Rome in a chariot drawn by four white horses, which no general ever did before or after him. Indeed, this sort of carriage is esteemed sacred, and is appropriated to the king and father of the gods. The citizens, therefore, considered this unusual appearance of grandeur as an insult to them. But the greatest and most manifest cause of their hatred was his behavior with respect to the tenths of the spoils. It seems he had made a vow, as he marched to Veii, that if he took the city he would consecrate the tenths to Apollo. But when the city was taken, and came to be pillaged, he was either unwilling to interrupt his men, or in the hurry had forgotten his vow. A charge of fraud with respect to these spoils was brought against him, and the people were much exasperated. At length he quitted the city, a voluntary exile.

While he was absent the Gauls, under Brennus, besieged Rome and defeated the Romans near the river Allia, and they were compelled to retire into the capitol or citadel.

The third day after the battle Brennus arrived at the city with his army; and finding the gates opened and the walls destitute of guards, at first he had some apprehension of a stratagem or ambuscade, for he could not think the Romans had so entirely given themselves up to despair. But when he found it to be so in reality, he entered by the Colline gate, and took Rome, a little more than three hundred and sixty years after its foundation.

Camillus was re-elected dictator, and marched at the head of an army to the relief of the capitol. Meantime, some of the barbarians employed in the siege, happening to pass by the place where Pontius had made his way by night up to the capitol, observed many traces of his feet and hands, as he had worked himself up to the rock. Of this they informed the king, who coming and viewing it, for the present said nothing; but in the evening he assembled the lightest and most active of his men, who were the likeliest to climb any difficult height, and thus addressed them:—
"The enemy have themselves shown us a way to reach them, which we were ignorant of, and have proved that this rock is neither inaccessible nor untrod by human feet. What a shame would it be then, after having made a beginning, not to finish; and to quit the place as impregnable, when

the Romans themselves have taught us how to take it? Where it was easy for one man to ascend, it cannot be difficult for many, one by one; nay, should many attempt it together, they will find great advantage in assisting each other. In the mean time, I intend great rewards and honors for such as shall distinguish themselves on this occasion."

The Gauls readily embraced the king's proposal; and about midnight a number of them began to climb the rock in silence, which, though steep and craggy, proved more practicable than they expected. The foremost having gained the top, put themselves in order, and were ready to take possession of the wall, and to fall upon the guards, who were fast asleep; for neither man nor dog perceived their coming. However, there were certain sacred geese kept near Juno's temple, and at other times plentifully fed; but at this time, as corn and the other provisions that remained were scarce sufficient for the men, they were neglected and in poor condition. Geese are naturally quick of hearing, and soon alarmed at any noise; and as hunger kept them waking and uneasy, they immediately perceived the coming of the Gauls, and running at them with all the noise they could make, they awoke all the guards. The barbarians now perceiving they were discovered, advanced with loud shouts and great fury. The Romans in haste snatched up such weapons as came to hand, and acquitted themselves like men on this sudden emergency.

The Gauls were repulsed, and Camillus, coming up immediately with his army, defeated Brennus and entered Rome in triumph. A wonderful change took place in the minds of the people, who exhorted and encouraged each other to work, and they began to rebuild immediately, not in any order or upon a regular plan, but as inclination or convenience directed. By reason of this hurry the streets of Rome were narrow and intricate, and the houses badly laid out; for they tell us both the walls of the city and the streets were rebuilt within the compass of a year.

Soon after Camillus had been appointed dictator the sixth time the Gauls again marched against Rome, and he defeated them near the river Anio. He died of the plague B.C. 365.

PERICLES.

Note.—PERICLES (Athenian). Pericles was born of a noble and wealthy family. He was gifted with wonderful eloquence, and began to take part in public affairs about B.C. 469. He lost many of his friends and finally his favorite son Paralus, through the plague. Pericles was heart-broken and died after a lingering illness, B.C. 429.

THIS great Athenian general, statesman, and orator, was a son of Xanthippus and Agariste. His person was well formed, but his head was disproportionately long. For this reason almost all his statues have the head covered with a helmet, the statuaries choosing, I suppose, to hide that defect; but the Athenian poets called him Schinocephalus, or onion-head. And Teleclides says of him—

> "Now, in a maze of thought he ruminates
> On strange expedients, while his head, depressed
> With its own weight, sinks on his knees; and now
> From the vast caverns of his brain burst forth
> Storms and fierce thunders."

Damon, under the pretence of teaching him music, instructed him in politics, and he attended the lectures of Zeno on natural philosophy. But the philosopher with whom he was most intimately acquainted, who gave him that force and sublimity of sentiment superior to all the demagogues, was Anaxagoras. This was he whom the people of those times called "nous," or intelligence, either in admiration of his great understanding and knowledge of the works of nature, or because he was the first who clearly proved that the universe owed its formation neither to chance nor necessity.

Charmed with the company of this philosopher, and instructed by him in the sublimest sciences, Pericles acquired not only an elevation of sentiment, and a loftiness and purity of style, far removed from the low expression of the vulgar, but likewise a gravity of countenance which relaxed not into laughter, a firm and even tone of voice, an easy deportment, and a decency of dress, which no vehemence of speaking ever put into disorder. These things, and others of the like nature, excited admiration in all who saw him.

Anaxagoras also cured him of superstition,

and taught him to be patient under injuries. His eloquence improved with his knowledge of philosophy, and from the force of it he was surnamed Olympias. The strokes of satire, both serious and ludicrous, in the comedies of those times, indicate that this title was given him chiefly on account of his eloquence; for they tell us that in his harangues he thundered and lightened, and that his tongue was armed with thunder. Thucydides is said to have given a pleasant account of the force of his eloquence. Thucydides was a great and respectable man, who, for a long time, opposed the measures of Pericles; and when Archidamus, one of the kings of Lacedæmon, asked him, "Which was the best wrestler, Pericles or he?" he answered, "When I throw him he says he was never down, and he persuades the very spectators to believe so." Yet such was the solicitude of Pericles, when he had to speak in public, that he always first addressed a prayer to the gods—"That not a word might unawares escape him unsuitable to the occasion."

Thucydides represents the administration of Pericles as favoring aristocracy, and tells us that though the government was called democratical, it was really in the hands of one who had engrossed the whole authority. Many other writers likewise inform us that by him the people were first indulged with a division of lands, were treated at the public expense with theatrical diversions, and were paid for the most common services to the State. By the constructing of great edifices, which required many arts and a long time to finish them, the mechanics had equal pretensions to be paid out of the treasury (though they stirred not out of the city) with the mariners and soldiers, guards and garrisons; for the different materials, such as stone, brass, ivory, gold, ebony, and cypress, furnished employment to carpenters, masons, braziers, goldsmiths, painters, turners, and other artificers. The conveyance of the materials by sea employed merchants and sailors, and by land wheelwrights, wagoners, carriers, ropemakers, leather-cutters, paviors, and iron founders. Every art had a number of the lower people ranged in proper subordination to execute it, like soldiers under the command of a general, and thus, by the exercise of these different trades, plenty was diffused among persons of every rank and condition. Works were thus raised of an astonishing magnitude and inimitable beauty and perfection, every architect striving to surpass the magnificence of the design with the elegance of the execution; yet still the most wonderful circumstance was the expedition with which they were completed. Many edifices, each of which seems to have required the labor of several successive ages, were finished during the administration of one prosperous man.

Pericles was so proud of these buildings that, when the people complained of the cost, he offered to be at the whole expense himself, if he might be allowed to inscribe his own name on them. He was particularly attentive to his finances. He used to turn a whole year's produce into money altogether, and with this he bought, from day to day, all manner of necessaries at the market; but this way of living was not agreeable to his sons when grown up, and the allowance he made the women did not appear to them a generous one. They complained of a pittance daily measured out with scrupulous economy, which admitted of none of those superfluities so common in great houses and wealthy families, and they could not bear to think of the expenses being so nicely adjusted to the income.

His chief merit in war was the safety of his measures. He never willingly engaged in any uncertain or very dangerous expedition, nor had any ambition to imitate those generals who are admired as great men because their rash enterprises have been attended with success; he always told the Athenians "that as far as their fate depended upon him they should be immortal."

Pericles, on his return to Athens after the reduction of Samos, celebrated in a splendid manner the obsequies of his countrymen who fell in that war, and pronounced himself the funeral oration, usual on such occasions. This gained him great applause; and when he came down from the rostrum the women paid their respects to him, and presented him with crowns and chaplets, like a champion just returned victorious from the lists.

Ion informs us that he was highly elated with this conquest, and scrupled not to say, "That

Agamemnon spent ten years in reducing one of the cities of the barbarians, whereas he had taken the richest and most powerful city among the Ionians in nine months."

During the first expedition of the Peloponnesian war Pericles showed his care for his soldiers by many careful maneuvers. As to those that were eager for an engagement and uneasy at his slow proceedings, he endeavored to bring them to reason by observing, "That trees when lopped will soon grow again, but when men are cut off the loss is not easily repaired." On one occasion an eclipse of the sun threw his soldiers into the greatest consternation. Pericles was on board his galley, and observing that the pilot was much astonished and perplexed, took his cloak, and having covered his eyes with it, asked him, "If he found anything terrible in that, or considered it as a sad presage?" Upon his answering in the negative, he said, "Where is the difference then between this and the other, except that something bigger than my cloak causes the eclipse?"

Pericles died of the plague, 429 B.C. When he was at the point of death, his surviving friends and the principal citizens sitting about his bed discoursed together concerning his extraordinary virtue, and the great authority he had enjoyed, and enumerated his various exploits and the number of his victories; for, while he was commander-in-chief, he had erected no less than nine trophies to the honor of Athens. These things they talked of, supposing that he attended not to what they said, but that his senses were gone. He took notice, however, of every word they had spoken, and thereupon delivered himself audibly as follows:— "I am surprised that while you dwell upon and extol these acts of mine, though fortune had her share in them, and many other generals have performed the like, you take no notice of the greatest and most honorable part of my character, namely, that no Athenian, through my means, ever put on mourning."

FABIUS MAXIMUS.

Note.—FABIUS MAXIMUS (Roman). The Fabii were an illustrious Roman family divided into many branches. Fabius Maximus Verrucosus is considered the greatest of the family. He was surnamed "Cunctator," the temporizer, which art of war he exemplified successfully in the conflict he sustained with Hannibal. He died B.C. 203.

THE founder of the family of the Fabii, one of the most numerous and illustrious in Rome, was Fabius, a son of Hercules. Fabius Maximus, of whom we are writing, was the fourth in descent. He had the surname of Verrucosus, from a small wart on his upper lip. He was likewise called Ovicula, from the mildness and gravity of his behavior when a boy. Nay, his composed demeanor, and his silence, his caution in engaging in the diversions of the other boys, the slowness and difficulty with which he took up what was taught him, together with the submissive manner in which he complied with the proposals of his comrades, brought him under the suspicion of stupidity and foolishness with those who did not thoroughly know him. Yet a few there were who perceived that his composedness was owing to the solidity of his manner, and who discerned withal a magnanimity and lion-like courage in his nature. In a short time, when application to business drew him out, it was obvious that his seeming inactivity was a command which he had of his passions, that his cautiousness was prudence, and that that which had passed for heaviness and insensibility was really an immovable firmness of soul. He saw what an important concern the administration was, and in what wars the republic was frequently engaged, and therefore by exercise prepared his body, considering its strength as a natural armor. At the same time he improved his powers of persuasion, as the engines by which the people are to be moved. In his eloquence there was nothing of affectation, no empty plausible elegance, but it was full of that good sense which was peculiar to him, and had a sententious force and depth, said to have resembled that of Thucydides.

Fabius Maximus was five times consul; and in his first consulship was honored with a triumph for the victory he gained over the Ligurians, who, being defeated by him in a set battle, with the loss of a great number of men, were driven behind the Alps, and kept from such inroads and ravages as they used to make in the neighboring provinces.

Hannibal having invaded Italy, and gained the battle of Trebia, advanced through Tuscany, laying waste the country, and striking Rome itself with terror and astonishment. This desolation was announced by signs and prodigies,—some familiar to the Romans, as that of thunder for instance, and others equally strange and unaccountable. For it was said that certain shields sweated blood; that bloody corn was cut at Antium; that red-hot stones fell from the air; that the Falerians saw the heavens open, and many billets fall, upon one of which these words were very legible, "Mars brandisheth his arms." Fabius paid but little regard to prodigies, as too absurd to be believed, notwithstanding the great effect they had upon the multitude. But being informed how small the numbers of the enemy were and of the want of money, he advised the Romans to have patience,—not to give battle to a man who led on an army hardened by many conflicts for this very purpose, but to send succor to their allies, and to secure the towns that were in their possession, until the vigor of the enemy expired of itself, like a flame for want of fuel.

He could not, however, prevail upon Flaminius. That general declared he would never suffer the war to approach Rome; nor, like Camillus of old, dispute within the walls who should be the master of the city. He therefore ordered the tribunes to draw out the forces, and mounted his horse, but was thrown headlong off, the horse, without any visible cause, being seized with a fright and trembling; yet he persisted in his resolution of marching out to meet Hannibal, and drew up his army near the lake called Thrasymenus in Tuscany.

While the armies were engaged there happened an earthquake, which overturned whole cities, changed the course of rivers, and tore off the tops of mountains; yet not one of the combatants was in the least sensible of that violent motion. Flaminius himself, having greatly signalized his strength and valor, fell, and with him the bravest of his troops. The rest being routed, a great carnage ensued; full fifteen thousand were slain, and as many taken prisoners.

Fabius was then chosen dictator, but instead of immediately giving battle to Hannibal he encamped in the mountains and watched the enemy. When they rested he did the same, and when they were in motion he showed himself upon the height at such a distance as not to be compelled to fight, but yet near enough to keep the enemy in perpetual alarm. These apparently dilatory proceedings exposed Fabius to contempt, even in his own army. His opponents asked in derision, "Whether he intended to take his army up into heaven, as he had bidden adieu to the world below, or whether he would screen himself from the enemy with clouds and fogs?" When the dictator's friends brought him an account of this and similar aspersions, and exhorted him to wipe them off by risking a battle,— "In that case," said he, "I should be of a more dastardly spirit than they represent me, if, through fear of insults and reproaches, I should depart from my own resolution. But to fear for my country is not a disagreeable fear. That man is unworthy of such a command as this who shrinks under calumnies and slanders, and complies with the humor of those whom he ought to govern, and whose folly and rashness it is his duty to restrain."

One of the stratagems of Hannibal during the maneuvring is singularly interesting. The contrivance was this: he caused two thousand oxen, which he had in his camp, to have torches and dry bavins well fastened to their horns. These, in the night, upon a signal given, were to be lighted, and the oxen to be driven to the mountains, near the narrow pass that was guarded by Fabius. While those that had it in charge were thus employed, he decamped, and marched slowly forward. So long as the fire was moderate, and burnt only the torches and bavins, the oxen moved softly on, as they were driven up the hills; and the shepherds and herdsmen on the adjacent heights took them for an army that marched in order with lighted torches. But when the animals' horns were burnt to the roots, and the fire pierced to the quick, terrified, and mad with pain, they no longer kept any certain route, but ran up the hills, with their foreheads and horns flaming, and setting everything on fire that came in their way. The Romans who guarded the pass were astonished; for the oxen appeared to them like a great number of men running up and down with torches, which scattered fire on every side. In their fears, of course, they concluded that they should be attacked and surrounded by the enemy; for which reason they quitted the pass, and fled to the main body in the camp. Immediately Hannibal's light-armed troops took possession of the outlet, and the rest of his forces marched safely through, loaded with a rich booty.

The general in command of the Roman cavalry was named Minucius. He was very eager to bring on an engagement with Hannibal; and, contrary to the orders of Fabius, he did so, and partly defeated the enemy. This success so pleased the Romans that they elected Minucius dictator with Fabius, and it was proposed that the dictators should have the command of the army alternately; but Fabius divided the forces, and gave the command of one half to Minucius, who was soon drawn into an engagement by Hannibal, and defeated. Fabius had expected the result, and was waiting at hand with his half of the army, and, advancing at the right moment, compelled Hannibal to retreat.

After the battle, Fabius, having collected the spoils of such Carthaginians as were left dead upon the field, returned to his post; nor did he let fall one haughty or angry word against his colleague. As for Minucius, having called his men together, he thus expressed himself:—
"Friends and fellow-soldiers, not to err at all in the management of great affairs is above the wisdom of men; but it is the part of a prudent and good man to learn, from his errors and miscarriages,

to correct himself for the future. For my part, I confess that though fortune has frowned upon me a little, I have much to thank her for. For what I could not be brought to be sensible of in so long a time, I have learned in the small compass of one day,—that I know ot how to command, but have need to be under the direction of another. From this moment I bid adieu to the ambition of getting the better of a man whom it is an honor to be foiled by. In all other respects the dictator shall be your commander; but in the due expressions of gratitude to him, I will be your leader still by being the first to show an example of obedience and submission."

He then marched to the camp of Fabius, and thus addressed himself to the dictator:—"You have this day Fabius, obtained two victories, one over the enemy by your valor, the other over your colleague by your prudence and humanity. By the former you saved us, by the latter you have instructed us; and Hannibal's victory over us is not more disgraceful than yours is honorable and salutary to us. I call you 'Father,' not knowing a more honorable name, and am more indebted to you than to my real father. To him I owe my being, but to you the preservation of my life, and the lives of all these brave men."

Fabius Maximus did not live to hear of the overthrow of Hannibal, or to see the prosperity of his country re-established; for about the time that Hannibal left Italy he fell sick and died. The expense of Fabius' funeral was not defrayed out of the Roman treasury, but every citizen contributed a small piece of money toward it; not that he died without effects, but that the Romans might bury him as the father of the people, and that the honors paid him at his death might be suitable to the dignity of his life.

ALCIBIADES.

Note.—ALCIBIADES (Greek). Alcibiades was born about 450 B.C. and descended on both sides from the most illustrious families of his country. Inheriting great wealth, endowed with remarkable attractiveness of person and brilliant mental powers, he could not fail to become a potent factor in the counsels and fortunes of Athens. The date and particulars of his death will be found in the sketch which follows.

ALCIBIADES was descended from Ajax. His father was Clinias, who had gained great honor in the sea-fight of Artemisium, where he fought in a galley fitted out at his own expense. By reason of the natural vigor of his constitution, and by his happy disposition, he long retained his youthful beauty.

He had a lisping in his speech, which became him, and gave a graceful and persuasive turn to his discourse. His manners were far from being uniform; nor is it strange that they varied according to the many vicissitudes and wonderful turns of his fortune. He was naturally a man of strong passions; but his ruling passion was an ambition to contend and overcome. This appears from what is related of his sayings when a boy. When hard pressed in wrestling, to prevent his being thrown he bit the hands of his antagonist, who let go his hold, and said, "Alcibiades, you bite like a woman." "No," said he, "like a lion."

One day he was playing at dice with other boys in the street; and when it came to his turn to throw, a loaded wagon came up. At first he called to the driver to stop, because he was to throw in the way over which the wagon was to pass. The rustic disregarding him and driving on, the other boys broke away; but Alcibiades threw himself upon his face directly before the wagon, and stretching himself out bade the fellow drive on if he pleased. Upon this he was so startled that he stopped his horses, while those who saw it ran up to him in terror.

In the course of his education he willingly took the lessons of his other masters; but refused learning to play upon the flute, which he looked upon as a mean art and unbecoming a gentleman.

"Playing upon the lyre," he would say, "has nothing in it that disorders the features or form, but a man is hardly to be known by his most intimate friends when he plays upon the flute. Besides, the lyre does not hinder the performer from speaking or accompanying it with a song, whereas the flute so engages the mouth and the breath that it leaves no possibility of speaking."

Many persons of rank made their court to Alcibiades, but it is evident that they were charmed and attracted by the beauty of his person. Socrates was the only one whose regards were fixed upon the mind, and bore witness to the young man's virtue and ingenuity, the rays of which he could distinguish through his fine form; and fearing lest the pride of riches and high rank, and the crowd of flatterers, both Athenians and strangers, should corrupt him, he used his best endeavors to prevent it, and took care that so hopeful a plant should not lose its fruit and perish in the very flower.

Alcibiades was fond of animals, and he was famed for his breed of horses and the number of his chariots; for no one besides himself, whether private person or king, ever sent seven chariots at one time to the Olympic games. The first, the second, and the fourth prizes, according to Thucydides, or the third, as Euripides relates it, he bore away at once, which exceeds everything performed by the most ambitious in that way. Euripides thus celebrates his success:—

> "Great son óf Clinias, I record thy glory,
>   First on the dusty plain
>   The threefold prize to gain;
> What hero boasts thy praise in Grecian story?
> Twice does the trumpet's voice proclaim
> Around the plausive cirque thy honor'd name:
>   Twice on thy brow was seen
>   The peaceful olive's green,
> The glorious palm of easy purchased fame."

His prodigious liberality, the games he exhibited, and the other extraordinary instances of his munificence to the people, the glory of his ancestors, the beauty of his person, and the force of his eloquence, together with his heroic strength, his valor, and experience in war, so gained upon the Athenians that they connived at his errors, and spoke of them with all imaginable tenderness, calling them sallies of youth and good-humored frolics.

Notwithstanding his popularity and success as a soldier, his enemies found cause of complaint. The information against him ran thus:—"Thessalus, the son of Cimon, of the ward of Lacias, accuseth Alcibiades, the son of Clinias, of the ward of Scambonis, of sacrilegiously offending the goddesses Ceres and Proserpine by counterfeiting their mysteries, and showing them to his companions in his own house. Wearing such a robe as the high-priest does while he shows the holy things, he called himself high-priest, as he did Polytion, torch-bearer, and Theodorus of the ward of Phygea, herald; and the rest of his companions he called persons initiated and brethren of the secret; herein acting contrary to the rules and ceremonies established by the Eumolpidæ, the heralds and priests at Eleusis." As he did not appear they condemned him, confiscated his goods, and ordered all the priests and priestesses to pronounce an execration against him.

He regained his popularity, and after many creditable military exploits he was defeated by Lysander, who destroyed the Athenian fleet and took the city of Athens. He established there the "thirty tyrants," one of whom, Critias by name, exhorted Lysander to have Alcibiades killed. Those who were sent to assassinate him, not daring to enter his house, surrounded it and set it on fire. As soon as he perceived it he got together large quantities of clothes and hangings, and threw them upon the fire to choke it; then having wrapped his robe about his left hand, and taking his sword in his right, he sallied through the fire, and got safe out before the stuff which he had thrown upon it could catch fire. At sight of him the barbarians dispersed, not one of them daring to wait for him, or to encounter him hand to hand; but, standing at a distance, they pierced him with their darts and arrows. Thus fell Alcibiades, at the age of forty-six, in the year B.C. 404.

CAIUS MARCIUS CORIOLANUS.

Note.—CAIUS MARCIUS CORIOLANUS (Roman). Caius Marcius was a famous legendary hero of Rome. His banishment was decreed in 491 B.C. Traditions differ as to his death. It is claimed by some that he was assassinated, while others assert that he lived to an old age among the Volscians.

CAIUS MARCIUS was brought up by his mother in her widowhood. The loss of a father, though attended with other disadvantages, is shown by him to be no hindrance to a man's improving in virtue and attaining to a distinguished excellence, though bad men sometimes allege it as an excuse for their corrupt lives. His undaunted courage and firmness of mind excited him to many great actions, and carried him through them with honor; but, at the same time, the violence of his passions, his spirit of contention, and excessive obstinacy, rendered him untractable and disagreeable in conversation; so that those very persons who saw with admiration his soul unshaken with pleasures, toils, and riches, and allowed him to be possessed of the virtues of temperance, justice, and fortitude, yet, in the councils and affairs of State, could not endure his imperious temper and that savage manner which was too haughty for a republic. Indeed, there is no other advantage to be had from a liberal education equal to that of polishing and softening our nature by reason and discipline; for that produces an evenness of behavior, and banishes from our manners all extremes.

The Romans at that time were engaged in several wars, and fought many battles, and there was not one that Marcius returned from without some honorary crown, some ennobling distinction. The end which others proposed in their acts of valor was glory; but he pursued glory because the acquisition of it delighted his mother; for when she was witness to the applauses he received, when she saw him crowned, when she embraced him with tears of joy, then it was that he reckoned himself at the height of honor and felicity.

He was called Coriolanus for his gallant behavior at Corioli. Soon afterward Marcius stood for the consulship. It was the custom for those who were candidates for such a high office to solicit and caress the people in the forum, and at those times to be clad in a loose gown without the tunic. That humble dress was thought more suitable for suppliants, and it was convenient for showing their wounds, as so many tokens of valor. It was not from any suspicion the citizens then had of bribery that they required the candidates to appear before them ungirt, and without any close garment, when they came to beg their votes; since it was much later than this, and indeed many ages after, that buying and selling stole in, and money came to be a means of gaining an election. Then, corruption reaching also the tribunals and the camps, arms were subdued by money, and the commonwealth was changed into a monarchy. It was a shrewd saying, whoever said it, "That the man who first ruined the Roman people was he who first gave them treats and gratuities."

When, therefore, Marcius showed the wounds and scars he had received in the many glorious battles he had fought for seventeen years successively, the people were struck with reverence for his virtue, and agreed to choose him consul. But when the day of election came the common people altered their minds, their kindness was turned to envy and indignation, and they rejected Marcius. Ultimately he was tried for "treason against the commonwealth, in designing to set himself up as a tyrant," and being condemned by a majority of three tribes he was doomed to perpetual banishment.

The pride of Coriolanus would not permit him to make his court to those who were capable of conferring honors upon him; and at the same time his ambition filled him with regret and indignation when they passed him by. This, then, is the blamable part of his character; all the rest is great and glorious. In point of temperance and disregard of riches he is fit to be compared with the most illustrious examples of integrity in Greece.

TIMOLEON.

Note.—TIMOLEON (Greek). Timoleon was a general and statesman. With the assistance of his brother Satyrus, he slew his elder brother Timophanes, who aimed at the sovereign power. He died at Syracuse 337 B.C.

THIS celebrated Corinthian was of a noble family. His father was Timodemus, and his mother Demariste. His love of his country was remarkable, and so was the mildness of his disposition, saving that he bore an extreme hatred to tyrants and wicked men. His natural abilities for war were so happily tempered, that, as an extraordinary prudence was seen in the enterprises of his younger years, so an undaunted courage distinguished his declining age.

Timoleon's most celebrated military exploit was the expedition against Syracuse. Scarce three thousand out of ten times that number took up arms, and ventured to follow Timoleon. The mercenaries were in number four thousand, and of them about a thousand gave way to their fears when upon the march, and turned back, saying, that "Timoleon must be mad, or in his dotage, to go against an army of seventy thousand men with only five thousand foot and a thousand horse; and to draw his handful of men, too, eight days' march from Syracuse, by which means there could be no refuge for those that fled, nor burial for those that fell in battle."

Timoleon considered it as an advantage that these cowards discovered themselves before the engagement; and having encouraged the rest, he led them hastily to the banks of the Crimesus, where he was told the Carthaginians were drawn together. But as he was ascending a hill, at the top of which the enemy's camp and all their vast forces would be in sight, he met some mules loaded with parsley; and his men took it into their heads that it was a bad omen, because the sepulchers are usually crowned with parsley; and thence the proverb with respect to one that is dangerously ill, "Such a one has need of nothing but parsley." To deliver them from this superstition, and to remove the panic, Timoleon ordered the troops to halt, and making a speech suitable to the occasion, observed, among other things, "That crowns were brought them before the victory, and offered themselves of their own accord;" for the Corinthians, from all antiquity, having looked upon a wreath of parsley as sacred, crowned the victors with it at the Isthmian games.

He ascribed all his successes to fortune; he

often said he was highly indebted to that goddess. In his house he built a chapel, and offered sacrifices to Chance, and dedicated the house itself to Fortune; for the Syracusans had given him one of the best houses in the city, as a reward for his services, and provided him, besides, a very elegant and agreeable retreat in the country. There it was that he spent most of his time, with his wife and children, whom he had sent for from Corinth; for he never returned home. He took no part in the troubles of Greece, nor exposed himself to public envy—the rock which great generals commonly split upon in their insatiable pursuit of honor and power; but he remained in Sicily, enjoying the blessings he had established, and of which the greatest of all was to see so many cities and so many thousands of people happy through his means.

He died at a good age, and was honored with a public funeral, being described in the funeral oration as "the man who had destroyed tyrants, subdued barbarians, re-peopled great cities which had lain desolate, and who had restored to the Sicilians their laws and privileges."

PAULUS ÆMILIUS.

Note.—PAULUS ÆMILIUS (Roman). This Roman general belonged to a noble family. At the age of forty-six he held the office of consul and was sixty years old when he accepted the command of the armies sent against Perseus, king of Macedon. He afterward served as censor. He was born 228 B.C., and died universally regretted, at the age of sixty-eight.

PAULUS ÆMILIUS was so named from the peculiar charm and gracefulness of his elocution. He was supposed to be a descendant of Numa.

It was the custom for those that were appointed to the consulship to make their acknowledgments to the people in an agreeable speech from the rostrum. Æmilius, having assembled the citizens on this occasion, told them,—"He had applied for his former Consulship because he wanted a command; but this time they had applied to him, because they wanted a commander; and, therefore, at present he did not hold himself obliged to them. If they could have the war better directed by another, he would readily quit the employment; but if they placed their confidence in him, he expected they would not interfere with his orders, or propagate idle reports, but provide in silence what was necessary for the war; for if they wanted to command their commanders their expeditions would be more ridiculous than ever." It is not easy to express how much reverence this speech procured him from the citizens, and what high expectations it produced. They rejoiced that they had passed by the smooth-tongued candidates, and made choice of a general who had so much freedom of speech and such dignity of manner.

Paulus Æmilius by good generalship defeated Perseus, king of Macedonia, who was taken prisoner. For this success at the battle of Pydna Æmilius was voted a triumph, which was carried out after this manner:—In every theater, or circus, as they called it, where equestrian games used to be held, in the forum, and other parts of the city, which were convenient for seeing the procession, the people erected scaffolds, and on the day of the triumph were all dressed in white. The temples were set open, adorned with garlands, and smoking with incense. Many lictors and other officers compelled the disorderly crowd to make way, and opened a clear passage. The triumph took up three days. On the first were exhibited the images, paintings, and colossal statues taken from the enemy, and carried in two hundred and fifty chariots. Next day the richest and most beautiful of the Macedonian arms were brought up in a great number of wagons. These glittered with new furbished brass and polished steel; and though they were piled with great art and judgment, yet seemed to be thrown together promiscuously; helmets being placed upon shields, breast-plates upon greaves, Cretan targets, Thracian bucklers, and quivers of arrows, huddled among the horses' bits, with the points of naked swords and long pikes appearing through on every side. All these arms were tied together with such a just liberty, that room was left for them to clatter as they were drawn along, and the clank of them was so harsh and terrible, that they were not seen without dread, though among the spoils of the conquered. After the carriages loaded with arms, walked three thousand men, who carried the silver money in seven hundred and fifty vessels, each of which contained three talents, and was borne by four men. Others brought bowls, horns, goblets, and cups, all of silver, disposed in such order as would make the best show, and valuable not only for their size but the depth of the basso-relievo. On the third day, early in the morning, first came up the trumpets, not with such airs as are used in a procession of solemn entry, but with such as the Romans sound when they animate their troops to the charge. These were followed by a hundred and twenty fat oxen, with their horns gilded, and set off with ribbons and garlands. The young men who led these victims were girded with belts of curious workmanship; and after them came the boys who carried the gold and silver vessels for the sacrifice. Next the persons who carried the gold coin, in vessels which held three talents each, like those that contained the silver, and which were to the number of seventy-seven. Then followed those that bore the consecrated bowl, of ten talents weight, which Æmilius had caused to be made of gold, and adorned with precious stones; and those that exposed to view the cups of Antigonus of Seleucus, and such as were of the make of the famed artist Shericles, together with the gold plate that had been used at Perseus' table. Immediately after was to be seen the chariot of that prince, with his armor upon it, and his diadem upon that; at a little distance his children were led captive, attended by a great number of governors, masters, and preceptors, all in tears, who stretched out their hands by way of supplication to the spectators, and taught the children to do the same. There were two sons and one daughter, all too young to be much affected with the greatness of their misfortunes. This insensibility of theirs made the change of their condition more pitiable; in so much that Perseus passed on almost without notice. So fixed were the eyes of the Romans upon the children, from pity of their fate, that many of them shed tears, and till they were gone by none tasted the joy of the triumph without a mixture of pain. Behind the children and their train walked Perseus himself, clad all in black, and wearing sandals of the fashion of his country. He had the appearance of a man who was overwhelmed with terror, and whose reason was almost staggered with the weight of his misfortunes. He was followed by a great number of friends and favorites, whose countenances were oppressed with sorrow, and who, by fixing their weeping eyes continually upon their prince, testified to the spectators that it was his lot which they lamented, and that they were regardless of their own. Next were carried four hundred coronets of gold, which the cities had sent Æmilius, along with their embassies, as compliments on his victory. Then came the Consul himself, riding in a magnificent chariot—a man, exclusive of the pomp of power, worthy to be seen and admired; but his good mien was now set off with a purple robe interwoven with gold, and he held a branch of laurel in his right hand. The whole army likewise carried boughs of laurel, and divided into bands and companies, followed the general's chariot. Some sang satirical songs usual on such occasions, and some chanted odes of victory.

He died B.C. 160, having attained to everything that is supposed to contribute to the happiness of man.

PELOPIDAS.

Note.—PELOPIDAS (Theban). After the return of Pelopidas as ambassador to the court of Persia, he assumed command of the forces sent to the relief of Thessaly, and, as stated by Plutarch, was slain in battle B.C. 364.

PELOPIDAS, the son of Hippoclus, was of an illustrious family of Thebes. Brought up in affluence, and coming in his youth to a great estate, he applied himself to relieve such necessitous persons as deserved his bounty, to show that he was really master, not the slave, of his riches.

Pelopidas married into a noble family, and had several children; but setting no greater value upon money than before, and devoting all his time to the concerns of the commonwealth, he impaired his substance; and when his friends admonished him, that money, which he neglected, was a very necessary thing,—"It is necessary, indeed," said he, "for Nicodemus, there," pointing to a man that was both lame and blind.

Epaminondas and he were both equally inclined to every virtue, but Pelopidas delighted more in the exercises of the body, and Epaminondas in the improvement of the mind. The one diverted himself in the wrestling ring or in hunting, while the other spent his hours of leisure in hearing or reading philosophy. Among the many things that reflected glory upon both, there was nothing which men of sense so much admired as that strict and inviolable friendship which existed between them from first to last, in all the high posts which they held, both military and civil.

In conjunction with Epaminondas he won a splendid victory at Leuctra, and the two friends were thereupon appointed joint governors of Bœotia. They drove the Spartans out of Messenia, and re-established the ancient inhabitants. Pelopidas was then sent to Macedonia as arbitrator between Alexander and Ptolemy, and afterwards went as ambassador to the Persian Court, where he was highly honored by Artaxerxes. He was killed in battle B. C. 364.

MARCELLUS.

Note.—MARCELLUS (Roman). Marcellus was the name of several noble Roman families. The striking death of Marcus Claudius Marcellus, as described by Plutarch, took place B.C. 208.

MARCUS CLAUDIUS MARCELLUS, who was five times consul, was the son of Marcus, and the first of his family that bore the surname of Marcellus, that is, *Martial*. He had, indeed, a great deal of military experience; his body was strong, his arm almost irresistible, and he was naturally inclined to war. But though impetuous and lofty in combat, on other occasions he was modest and humane. He was so far a lover of the Grecian learning and eloquence as to honor and admire those that excelled therein, though his employments prevented his making that progress in them which he desired.

The account of the siege of Syracuse is full of interest. Marcellus made his attacks both by sea and land,—Appius Claudius commanding the land forces, and himself the fleet, which consisted of sixty galleys, of five banks of oars, full of all sorts of arms and missile weapons. Besides these, he had a prodigious machine, carried upon eight galleys fastened together, with which he approached the walls, relying upon the number of his batteries and other instruments of war, as well as on his own great character. But Archimedes, the philosopher, despised all this, and confided in the superiority of his engines. He made for King Hiero all manner of engines and machines which could be used either for attack or defence in a siege. They were extremely serviceable to the Syracusans on the present occasion, who, with such a number of machines, had the advantage of their being directed by the inventor.

When the Romans attacked them, both by sea and land, they were struck dumb with terror, imagining they could not possibly resist such numerous forces and so furious an assault. But Archimedes soon began to play his engines, and they shot against the land forces all sorts of missiles, weapons, and stones of an enormous size, with so incredible a noise and rapidity, that nothing could stand before them; they overturned and crushed whatever came in their way, and spread terrible disorder throughout the ranks. On the side toward the sea were erected vast machines, shooting forth on a sudden, over the walls, huge beams with the necessary tackle, which striking with a prodigious force on the enemy's galleys, sank them at once; while other ships, hoisted up at the prows by iron grapples or hooks, like the beaks of cranes, and set on end, were plunged to the bottom of the sea. Others, again, by ropes and graplines, were drawn toward the shore, and after being whirled about, and dashed against the rocks that projected below the walls, were broken to pieces, and the crews perished. Very often a ship, lifted high above the sea, suspended and twirling in the air, presented a most dreadful spectacle. There it swung till the men were thrown out by the violence of the motion, and then it split against the walls, or sank on the engine's letting go its hold. As for the machine which Marcellus brought forward upon eight galleys, and which was called "Sambuca," on account of its likeness to the musical instrument of that name, whilst it was at a considerable distance from the walls, Archimedes discharged a stone of ten talents weight, and after that a second and a third, all which striking upon it with an amazing noise and force, shattered and totally disjointed it.

Marcellus, in this distress, drew off his galleys as fast as possible, and likewise sent orders to the land forces to retreat. He then called a council of war, in which it was resolved to come close to the walls, if it were possible, next morning before day; for Archimedes' engines, they thought, being very strong, and intended to act at a considerable distance, would then discharge the missiles over their heads, and if they were pointed at them when they were so near they would have no effect. But for this Archimedes had long been prepared, having by him engines fitted to all distances, with suitable weapons and shorter beams. Besides, he had caused holes to be made in the walls, in which he placed scorpions that did not carry far, but could be discharged very fast; and by these the enemy was galled, without knowing whence the missile came.

When, therefore, the Romans were got close to the walls, undiscovered, as they thought, they were welcomed with a shower of darts and huge pieces of rocks, which fell, as it were, perpendicularly upon their heads; for the engines played from every quarter of the walls. This obliged them to retire; and when they were at some distance, other shafts were shot at them in their retreat from the larger machines, which made terrible havoc among them, as well as greatly damaged their shipping. Archimedes had placed most of his engines under cover of the walls, so that the Romans, being infinitely distressed by an invisible enemy, seemed to fight against the gods.

Marcellus, however, got off and laughed at his own artillerymen and engineers, saying,—"Why do we not leave off contending with this mathematical Briareus, who, sitting on the shore, and acting as it were but in jest, has shamefully baffled our naval assault; and, in striking us with such a multitude of bolts at once, exceeds even the hundred-handed giants in the fable?" At last, the Romans were so terrified that if they saw but a rope or a stick put over the walls, they cried out that Archimedes was leveling some machine at them, and turned their backs and fled. Marcellus seeing this, gave up all thoughts of proceeding by assault, and leaving the matter to time, turned the siege into a blockade.

When at last the city was taken, Archimedes was found in his study engaged in some mathematical researches. His mind as well as his eye was so intent upon his diagram that he neither heard the tumultuous noise of the Romans nor perceived that the city was taken. A soldier suddenly entered his room, and ordered him to follow him to Marcellus; and Archimedes refusing to do it till he had finished his problem and brought his demonstration to bear, the soldier, in a passion, drew his sword and killed him. Marcellus was much concerned at his death, and bestowed many favors on his relatives.

A subsequent battle with Hannibal is thus described:—Both armies then engaged; and Hannibal, seeing no advantage gained by either, ordered his elephants to be brought forward into the first line, and to be pushed against the Romans. The shock caused great confusion at first in the Roman front; but Flavius, a tribune, snatching an ensign-staff from one of the companies, advanced, and with the point of it wounded the foremost elephant. The beast upon this turned back, and ran upon the second, the second upon the next that followed, and so on till they were all put in great disorder. Marcellus observing this, ordered his horse to fall furiously upon the enemy, and, taking advantage of the confusion already made, to rout them entirely. Accordingly, they charged with extraordinary vigor, and drove the Carthaginians to their entrenchments. The slaughter was dreadful; and the fall of the killed, and the plunging of the wounded elephants, contributed greatly to it. It is said that more than eight thousand Carthaginians fell in this battle; of the Romans not above three thousand were slain, but almost all the rest were wounded.

In a later battle Hannibal was successful, and Marcellus was caught in an ambuscade and killed. Hannibal, when he knew that Marcellus was dead, hastened to the place, and, standing over the body a long time, surveyed its size and mien, but without speaking one insulting word, or showing the least sign of joy, which might have been expected at the fall of so dangerous and formidable an enemy. At last, taking his signet from his finger, he caused the body to be magnificently attired and burned, and the ashes to be put in a silver urn, and then placed a crown of gold upon it.

ARISTIDES.

Note.—ARISTIDES (Athenian). This famous Athenian flourished in the fifth century B.C. He was twice banished, and died in poverty and exile B.C. 467.

ARISTIDES was an Athenian general, son of Lysimachus. Of all the virtues of Aristides, the people were most struck with his justice. Thus he, though a poor man and a commoner, gained the royal and divine title of "The Just," which kings and tyrants have never been fond of. It has been their ambition to be styled "Takers of cities," "Thunderbolts," or "Conquerors." Nay, some have chosen to be called "Eagles" and "Vultures," preferring the fame of power to that of virtue.

Aristides at first was loved and respected for his surname of "The Just," and afterwards envied as much; the latter, chiefly by the management of Themistocles, who gave it out among the people that Aristides had abolished the courts of judicature by drawing the arbitration of all causes to himself, and so was insensibly gaining sovereign power. The people, uneasy at finding any one citizen rising to such extraordinary honor and distinction, assembled at Athens from all the towns in Attica, and banished Aristides by the Ostracism—disguising their envy of his character under the specious pretence of guarding against tyranny.

The Ostracism was conducted in the following manner:—Every citizen took a piece of a broken pot, or a shell, on which he wrote the name of the person he wished to have banished, and carried it to a part of the market-place that was inclosed with wooden rails. The magistrates then counted the number of the shells, and if it amounted not to six thousand, the Ostracism stood for nothing; if it did, they sorted the shells, and the person whose name was found on the greatest number was declared an exile for ten years, but with permission to enjoy his estate. At the time that Aristides was banished, when the people were inscribing the names on the shells, it is reported that an illiterate burgher came to Aristides whom he took for some ordinary person, and giving him his shell, desired him to write "Aristides" upon it. The good man, surprised at the adventure, asked him,—"Whether Aristides had ever injured him?" "No," said he; "nor do I even know him; but it vexes me to hear him everywhere called 'The Just.'" Aristides made no answer, but took the shell, and having written his own name upon it, returned it. He was banished for ten years: but after three years, when Xerxes was marching through Thessaly and Bœotia to Attica, the Athenians recalled Aristides.

As to his death, some say it happened in Pontus, others that he died at Athens, full of days, honored and admired by his fellow-citizens.

CATO, THE CENSOR.

Note—CATO THE CENSOR (Roman). The date of Cato's birth was B.C. 234. He well deserved the name of Wise. He was elected consul in B.C. 195, and completed his brilliant military career at Thermopylæ. His election to the censorship took place B.C. 184. When he died, at the age of eighty-five, he left one hundred and fifty orations which are greatly admired.

PORCIUS CATO was born at Tusculum. Inured to labor and temperance, and brought up in camps, he had an excellent constitution, and was healthy and strong. He studied eloquence, because he considered it not only useful but necessary for every man who does not wish to live an obscure, inactive life. He was soon considered an able pleader and a good orator. He was not only so disinterested as to plead without fee or reward, but it appears that honor was his principal aim. But the height of his ambition was to be great in military matters. When he was but a youth he had fought in so many battles that his breast was covered with scars. In battle he stood firm, had a fierce look, and spoke to his enemy in a threatening and dreadful accent. He judged that such behavior often strikes an adversary with greater terror than the sword itself. He always marched on foot, carried his own weapons, and was attended by one servant only, who carried provisions. All the time he was in the army he usually drank nothing but water; but when almost burnt up with thirst he would ask for a little vinegar, or when his strength was exhausted he took a little wine. A nobleman of great power and eminence, named Valerius Flaccus, was so charmed with Cato's character that he encouraged him to go to Rome and apply himself to affairs of State. There he took Fabius Maximus as his example, and was the opponent of Scipio. He soon gained so much influence and authority by his eloquence that he was commonly called the Roman Demosthenes; but he was still more celebrated for his frugal manner of living. He has stated himself that he thought nothing cheap that was superfluous; that what a man has no need of is dear even at a penny; and that it is much better to have fields where the plow goes or cattle feed, than fine gardens and walks that require much watering and sweeping. It was a saying of his, "That wise men learn more from fools than fools from the wise; for the wise avoid the errors of fools, while fools do not profit by the example of the wise." Another of his sayings was, "That he liked a young man that blushed more than one that turned pale; and that he did not like a soldier who moved his hands in marching, and his feet in fighting, and who snored louder in bed than he shouted in battle."

He was a good father, a good husband, and an excellent economist. He chose his wife rather for her family than her fortune; persuaded that though both the rich and the high-born have their pride, yet women of good families are more ashamed of any base and unworthy action, and more obedient to their husbands in everything that is good and honorable. When he had a son born, no business, however urgent, except public affairs, could hinder him from being present while his wife washed and swaddled the infant; for she suckled it herself. Nay, she often gave the breast to the sons of her servants, to inspire them with a brotherly regard for her own. As soon as the dawn of understanding appeared, Cato took upon him the office of schoolmaster to his son, though he had a servant who was a good grammarian, and taught several other children. But he tells us he did not choose that his son should be reprimanded by a slave, or pulled by the ears if he happened to be slow in learning, or that he should be indebted to so mean a person for his education. He was, therefore, himself his preceptor in grammar, in law, and in the necessary exercises; for he taught him not only how to throw a dart, to fight hand-to-hand, and to ride, but to box, to endure heat and cold, and to swim the most rapid rivers.

He wrote a book concerning country affairs, in which, among other things, he gives rules for making cakes and preserving fruit; for he was desirous to be thought curious and particular in everything. He kept a better table in the country than in the town; for he always invited some of his acquaintances in the neighborhood to sup with him. With these he passed the time in cheerful conversation, making himself agreeable not only to those of his own age, but to the young. He looked upon the table as one of the best means of forming friendships; and at his the conversation generally turned upon the praises of great and excellent men among the Romans. As for the bad and the unworthy, no mention was made of them; for he would not allow in his company one word, either good or bad, to be said of such men.

The last service he is said to have done the public was the destruction of Carthage. The younger Scipio, indeed, gave the finishing stroke to that work, but it was undertaken chiefly by the advice and at the instance of Cato.

PHILOPŒMEN.

Note.—PHILOPŒMEN (Greek). Philopœmen, called the last of the Greeks, was born in Arcadia, B.C. 252. His death by poison, when a prisoner of the Messenians, took place B.C. 183.

PHILOPŒMEN, from a child, was fond of everything military, and readily entered into the exercises which tended to that purpose; those of riding, for instance, and handling of weapons. As he seemed well formed for wrestling, too, his friends and governors advised him to improve himself in that art; which gave him occasion to ask whether that might be consistent with his proficiency as a soldier? They told him the truth; that the habit of body and manner of life, the diet and exercise, of a soldier and a wrestler, were entirely different; that the wrestler must have much sleep and full meals, stated times of exercise and rest, every little departure from his rules being very prejudicial to him; whereas the soldier should be prepared for the most irregular changes of living, and should chiefly endeavor to bring himself to bear the want of food and sleep without difficulty. Philopœmen, hearing this, not only avoided and derided the exercise of wrestling himself, but afterward, when he came to be general, to the utmost of his power exploded the whole art, by every mark of disgrace and expression of contempt,—satisfied that it rendered persons who were the most fit for war quite useless and unable to fight on necessary occasions.

His leisure he spent either in the chase, which increased both his strength and activity, or in the tillage of the field. For he had a handsome estate, twenty furlongs from the city, to which he went every day after dinner, or after supper; and at night he threw himself upon an ordinary mattress and slept as one of the laborers. Early in the morning he rose and went to work along with his vine-dressers or plowmen; after which he returned to the town, and employed his time about the public affairs with his friends, and with the magistrates. What he gained in the wars he laid out upon horses or arms, or in redeeming captives. He was elected general of the Achæans the eighth time when he was seventy years of age, and he did not then think himself too old to command an army. He marched against the Messenians, but was captured and poisoned.

TITUS QUINCTIUS FLAMINIUS.

Note.—TITUS QUINCTIUS FLAMINIUS (Roman). This Roman general was made consul B.C. 198. His defeat of Philip at Cynoscephalæ, B.C. 197, terminated the Macedonian war. He went to Prusias, king of Bythnia, in B.C. 183 to demand the surrender of Hannibal who had taken refuge at the court. The death of Flaminius took place about B.C. 175.

THIS celebrated Roman general was, from his youth, trained to the profession of arms. His early successes in the wars inspired him with such lofty thoughts that, overlooking the ordinary previous steps by which young men ascend,

I mean the offices of tribune, prætor, and ædile, he aimed directly at the consulship. But the tribunes, Fulvius and Manlius, opposed him, insisting that is was a strange and unheard-of thing for a man so young, who was not yet initiated in the first mysteries of government, to intrude in contempt of the laws, into the highest office in the State. The senate referred the affair to the suffrages of the people; and the people elected him Consul, though he was not yet thirty years old.

Flaminius was successful in setting Greece free, and greatly prided himself in having done so. He dedicated some silver bucklers, together with his own shield, at Delphi; he put upon them the following inscription:—

> "Ye Spartan twins, who tamed the foaming steed,
> Ye friends, ye patrons of each glorious deed,
> Behold Flaminius, of Æneas' line,
> Presents this offering at your awful shrine.
> Ye sons of love, your generous paths he trod,
> And snatched from Greece each little tyrant's rod."

He offered also to Apollo a golden crown, with verses inscribed on it.

Hannibal was seventy years old when he was defeated at Zama by Scipio. Flaminius provoked him to destroy himself. Some say Hannibal wound his cloak about his neck and ordered his servant to put his knees upon his back, and pull with all his force, and not to leave off twisting till he had quite strangled him. Others tell us that, like Themistocles and Midas, he drank bull's blood. But Livy writes, that, having poison in readiness, he mixed it for a draught, and taking the cup in his hand, said,—"Let me deliver the Romans from their cares and anxieties, since they think it too tedious and dangerous to wait for the death of a poor hated old man. Yet shall not Titus gain a conquest worth envying, or suitable to the generous proceedings of his ancestors." Thus Hannibal is said to have died. When the news was brought to the senate, many in that august body were highly displeased. Flaminius appeared too officious and cruel in his precautions to procure the death of Hannibal, now tamed by his misfortunes, like a bird, that, through age, had lost its tail and feathers, and suffered to live so; and, as he had no orders to put him to death, it was plain that he did it out of a passion for fame, and to be mentioned in after-times as the destroyer of Hannibal.

PYRRHUS.

Note.—PYRRHUS (Greek). Pyrrhus ascended his father's throne 295 B.C. He made war on the Romans fourteen years later and was one of the most illustrious generals of the age in which he lived. The particulars of his death are given in the following sketch.

PYRRHUS was a renowned king of Epirus, who was descended from Hercules on his father's side, and from Achilles on his mother's. On the banishment of his father Æacides he was taken to the court of Glaucias, King of Illyricum, who brought him up, and succeeded in putting him on the throne of Epirus when he was quite a youth. Pyrrhus is described as having an air of majesty rather terrible than august. Instead of teeth in his upper jaw he had one continued bone, marked with small lines, resembling the divisions of a row of teeth. He was believed to have the power of curing the spleen, and it is asserted that this miraculous power was seated in the great toe of the right foot, for after his death, when his body was consumed by the fire, the toe was found untouched by the flames.

Neoptolemus succeeded in usurping the throne when Pyrrhus was about nineteen years old, but after a good deal of fighting he regained his kingdom. He then gladly accepted the invitation of the Tarentines to help them against the Romans. In his first battle with them his elephants obtained him the victory, for the Romans were frightened at their bulk and ferocity. The number of slain was so nearly equal on both sides that, though Pyrrhus was conqueror, he uttered the memorable saying, "Another such victory and we are undone." He next went against the Carthaginians, and obtained two victories and took many towns. He then renewed hostilities against the Romans at Tarentum, and was defeated by Curius. He left Italy much mortified that one of the descendants of Achilles should have been thus defeated. In Epirus he sought to regain his military renown, and began by attacking Antigonus, whom he conquered, and was once more raised to the throne of Macedonia. He afterward marched against Sparta, but was compelled to retreat to Argos. It was in this town that he met his death. His army reached the city at night, and got as far as the market-place, when it was found that the gate was not high enough to allow the elephants to pass under, and it was necessary to take off their towers. When the animals had passed through their towers were put on again. This took so much time that the citizens were aroused, and ran to the fort for safety. Meantime, the town was filled with soldiers, friends, and foes. Pyrrhus entered, and was welcomed by loud shouts. He pushed forward his cavalry, though they marched in danger from the number-of drains and sewers of which the city was full. Besides, in this nocturnal engagement it was impossible either to see what was done, or hear the orders that were given. The soldiers lost their way in the narrow streets, and the officers could not rally them, and daylight was anxiously waited for. At the first dawn, Pyrrhus was concerned to see the Aspis, or citadel, full of armed men; but his concern was changed into consternation when, amongst the statuary in the market-place, he saw a wolf and a bull in brass represented in the act of fighting; for he recollected an oracle which had foretold "that it was his destiny to die when he should see a wolf encountering a bull."

Pyrrhus, quite dispirited at the sight, and perceiving at the same time that nothing succeeded according to his hopes, thought it best to retreat. Fearing that the gates were too narrow, he sent orders to his son Helenus, who was left with the main body outside the town, to demolish part of the wall, and assist the retreat if the enemy tried to obstruct it. But the person whom he sent, mistaking the order in the hurry and tumult, and delivering it quite in a contrary sense, the young prince entered the gates with the rest of the elephants and the best of his troops, and marched to assist his father. Pyrrhus was now retiring, and while the market-place afforded room both to retreat and fight, he often faced about and repulsed the assailants. But when from that broad place he came to crowd into the narrow street leading to the gate, he fell in with those who were advancing to his assistance. It was in vain to call out to them to fall back; there were but few that could hear him; and such as did hear, and were most disposed to obey his orders, were pushed back by those who came pouring in behind. Besides, the largest of the elephants had fallen down in the gateway, and lying there and braying in a horrible manner, it stopped those who would have got out. And among the elephants already in the town, one named Nicon, striving to take up his master who was fallen off wounded, rushed against the party that was retreating, and overturned both friends and enemies promiscuously till he found the body, when he took it up with his trunk, and, carrying it on his tusks, returned in great fury, and trod down all before him. When they were thus pressing and crowded together, not a man could do anything singly; but the whole multitude, like one close compact body, rolled this way and that all together. They exchanged but few blows with the enemy either in front or rear, and the greatest harm they did was to themselves; for if any man drew his sword or leveled his pike, he could not recover the one or put up the other; the next person, therefore, whoever he happened to be, was necessarily wounded, and thus many of them fell by the hands of each other.

Pyrrhus, seeing the tempest rolling around him, took off the plume with which his helmet was distinguished, and gave it to one of his friends; then, trusting to the goodness of his horse, he rode in amongst the enemy who were harassing his rear, and it happened that he was wounded through the breast-plate with a javelin. The wound was rather slight than dangerous, but he turned against the man that gave it, who was an Argive of no note, the son of a poor old woman. This woman among others, looking at the fight from the roof of a house, beheld her son thus engaged. Seized with terror at the sight, she took up a large tile with both her hands, and threw it at Pyrrhus. The tile fell upon his head, and, notwithstanding his helmet, crushed the lower vertebræ of his neck. Darkness in a moment covered his eyes, his hands let go the reins, and he fell from his horse by the tomb of Licymnius. His head was cut off and carried to Antigonus B.C. 272.

Pyrrhus has been greatly extolled as a general,

not only by his friends but also by his enemies. The Romans praised him greatly, and he is stated to have said that if he had soldiers like the Romans he would have conquered all the nations of the world.

CAIUS MARIUS.

Note.—CAIUS MARIUS (Roman). Caius Marius was born about B.C. 157, probably at Cerretinum. Having entered the army he became known to Scipio Africanus. His great success caused him to be hailed "The Third Founder of Rome," and he was rewarded with a fifth consulate, followed by a sixth. He afterward became infamous because of his bloody prosecutions. While Consul for the seventh time, he died, as it is believed, from excessive indulgence in wine.

WE know of no third name of Caius Marius. Like some other Roman generals he was of poor parentage; but, forsaking the plow for the sword, he soon signalized himself as a soldier, under Scipio, at the siege of Numantia. He was elected Consul, and appointed to carry on the war against Jugurtha, whom he defeated.

Soon after this the Roman provinces were invaded by a band of barbarians from all parts, estimated at three hundred thousand men. Marius was sent against the Teutones. He came up with them at Aquæ Sextiæ, a short march from the Alps. There Marius prepared for battle, having pitched upon a place for his camp which was unexceptionable in point of strength, but afforded little water. By this circumstance, they tell us, he wanted to excite the soldiers to action ; and when many of them complained of thirst he pointed to a river which ran close by the enemy's camp, and told them, "That thence they must purchase water with their blood." "Why then," said they, "do you not lead us thither immediately, before our blood is quite parched up?" To which he answered in a softer tone, "I will lead you thither, but first let us fortify our camp."

The soldiers obeyed, though with some reluctance. But the servants of the army, being in great want of water both for themselves and their cattle, ran in crowds to the stream, some with pickaxes, some with hatchets, and others with swords and javelins, along with their pitchers; for they were resolved to have water, though they were obliged to fight for it. These at first were encountered by a small party of the enemy ; when some having bathed, were engaged at dinner, and others were still bathing, for there the country abounds in hot wells. This gave the Romans an opportunity of cutting off a number of them, while they were indulging themselves in those delicious baths, and charmed with the sweetness of the place. The cry of these brought others to their assistance ; so that it was now difficult for Marius to restrain the impetuosity of his soldiers, who were in pain for their servants. Besides the Ambrones, to the number of thirty thousand, who were the best troops the enemy had, and who had already defeated Manlius and Cæpio, were drawn out, and stood to their arms. Though they had overcharged themselves with eating, yet the wine they had drunk had given them fresh spirits; and they advanced, not in a wild and disorderly manner, or with a confused and inarticulate noise, but beating their arms at regular intervals, and all keeping time with the tune, they came on, crying out, "Ambrones!" "Ambrones!" This they did either to encourage each other or to terrify the enemy with their name. The Ligurians were the first of the Italians that moved against them; and when they heard the enemy cry "Ambrones," they echoed back the word, which was indeed their own ancient name. Thus the shout was often returned from one army to the other before they charged, and the officers on both sides joining in it, and striving which should pronounce the word loudest, added by this means to the courage and impetuosity of their troops.

The Ambrones were obliged to pass the river, and this broke their order; so that, before they could form again, the Ligurians charged the foremost of them, and thus began the battle. The Romans came to support the Ligurians; and pouring down from the higher ground, pressed the enemy so hard that they soon put them in disorder. Many of them jostling each other on the banks of the river, were slain there, and the river itself was filled with dead bodies. Those who got safe over not daring to make headway, were cut off by the Romans, as they fled to their camp and carriages. There the women, meeting them with swords and axes, and setting up a horrid and hideous cry, fell upon the fugitives, as well as the pursuers, the former as traitors and the latter as enemies. Mingling with the combatants, they laid hold on the Roman shields, catched at their swords with their naked hands, and obstinately suffered themselves to be hacked to pieces. It is computed that two hundred thousand of the barbarian forces were killed in this compaign. Next year the Cimbri were overthrown, and one hundred and forty thousand were killed, and sixty thousand taken prisoners by the Romans. Marius was then elected Consul for the sixth time, and soon after, in endeavoring to crush the power of Sylla, he laid the foundation of a civil war. He was obliged to fly to Africa for safety, where he was discovered. Sylla ordered him to be killed. No citizen would undertake this office; but a dragoon went up to him sword in hand, with an intent to dispatch him. The chamber in which he lay was somewhat gloomy, and a light, they tell you, glanced from the eyes of Marius, which darted on the face of the assassin; while, at the same time, he heard a solemn voice saying, "Dost thou dare to kill Marius?" Upon this the assassin threw down his sword and fled, crying, "I cannot kill Marius."

He died of fever, at the age of seventy.

LYSANDER.

Note.—LYSANDER (Spartan). Lysander lived in the fourth century B.C. His defeat of the Athenians under Antiochus, off the coast of Asia Minor, took place B.C. 407. His victory of Ægos Potamos, which virtually ended the Peloponnesian war, occurred two years later.

ARISTOCLITUS, the father of Lysander, is said not to have been of the royal line, but to be descended from the Heraclidæ by another family. As for Lysander, he was bred in poverty. No one conformed more freely to the Spartan discipline than he did. He had a firm heart, above yielding to the charms of any pleasure, except those which result from the honor and success gained by great actions. At Sparta they instilled into their children an early passion for glory, and taught them to be as much affected by disgrace as elated by praise.

Early in life Lysander ingratiated himself greatly with Cyrus the Younger, who presented him with ten thousand pieces of gold. With this money he increased the pay of his seamen, and by that means he made his navy so popular that the ships of the enemy were nearly emptied of men. Still he was afraid to give battle to Alcibiades personally, but as soon as that commander left the fleet in charge of Antiochus he fought and conquered.

In the next fight with the Athenians, which was at Ægos Potamos, Lysander had an army as well as a navy, and by waiting for a favorable opportunity he succeeded in completely defeating the enemy, taking one hundred and twenty ships. When he had fastened the captive galleys to his own, and plundered the camp, he returned to Lampsacus, accompanied with the flutes and songs of triumph. This great action cost him but little blood; in one hour he put an end to the Peloponnesian war, which lasted twenty-seven years. It had been diversified beyond all others by an incredible variety of events. This cruel war, which produced such vicissitudes of fortune, and destroyed more generals than all the wars of Greece put together, was terminated by the conduct and capacity of one man. Some, therefore, esteemed it the effect of a divine interposition. There were those who said that the stars of Castor and Pollux appeared on each side the helm of Lysander's ship when he first set out against the Athenians. Others thought that a stone, which, according to the common opinion, fell from heaven, was an omen of this overthrow. It is said that Anaxagoras had foretold that one of those bodies which are fixed in the vault of heaven would one day be loosened by some shock or convulsion of the whole machine, and fall to the earth; for he taught that the stars are not now in the places where they were originally; that, being of a stony substance and heavy, the light they give is caused only by the reflection and refraction of the surrounding ether; and that they are carried along and kept in their orbits by the rapid motion of the heavens, which from the beginning, when the cold, ponderous bodies were separated from the rest, hindered them from falling.

But there is another and more probable opinion which holds that falling stars are not emanations or detached parts of the elementary fire that go out the moment they are kindled; nor yet a quanity of air bursting out from some compression, and taking fire in the upper region; but that they are really heavenly bodies, which, from some relaxation of the rapidity of their motion, or by some irregular concussion, are loosened and fall, not so much upon the habitable part of the globe as into the ocean, which is the reason that their substance is seldom seen.

Lysander compelled the Athenians to pull down the fortifications and the long wall of the Piræus. He found a pretence to change the form of government and set up the thirty tyrants. He paid great compliments to the poets, and they in their turn covered him with fulsome flattery. He got to be extremely arrogant and cruel, and was killed in battle by the Haliartians, B.C. 394.

Among the other honors paid to the memory of Lysander, that which I am going to mention is none of the least. Some persons who had contracted themselves to his daughters in his lifetime, when they found he died poor, fell off from their engagements. The Spartans fined them for courting the alliance while they had riches in view, and breaking off when they discovered the poverty, which was the best proof of Lysander's probity and justice. It seems, at Sparta, there was a law which punished not only those who continued in a state of celibacy, or married too late, but those who married ill; and it was leveled chiefly at persons who married into rich rather than good families.

SYLLA (SULLA).

Note.—SYLLA (Roman). This Roman general, born B.C. 138, was one of the most debased of men, as he is graphically pictured by Plutarch. He became consul in his forty-ninth year and was made dictator of Rome B.C. 81. His frightful death occurred B.C. 78, when he was sixty years old.

THERE is very little that is creditable in the character of Lucius Cornelius Sylla. He gained his fame by his military achievements. He was born of poor parents. As to his figure, we have the whole of it in his statues, except his eyes. They were of a lively blue, fierce and menacing; and the ferocity of his aspect was heightened by his complexion, which was a strong red, interspersed with spots of white. From his complexion, they tell us, he had the name of Sylla; and an Athenian droll drew the following jest from it: "Sylla's a mulberry, strew'd o'er with meal." Nor is it foreign to make these observations upon a man who in his youth, before he emerged from obscurity, was such a lover of drollery that he spent his time with mimics and jesters, and went with them every length of riot. Nay, when in the height of his power, he would collect the most noted players and buffoons every day, and, in a manner unsuitable to his age and dignity, drink and join with them in licentious wit, while business of consequence lay neglected. Indeed, Sylla would never admit of anything serious at his table; and though at other times a man of business, and rather grave and austere in his manner, he would change instantaneously, whenever he had company, and begin a carousal; so that to buffoons and dancers he was the most affable man in the world, the most easy of access, and they molded him just as they pleased.

His passion for taking Athens was irresistibly violent; whether it was that he wanted to fight against that city's ancient renown, of which nothing but the shadow now remained; or whether he could not bear the scoffs and taunts with which Aristion, in all the wantonness of ribaldry, insulted him and Metellus from the walls.

The composition of this tyrant's heart was insolence and cruelty. He was the sink of all the follies and vices of Mithridates. Poor Athens, which had got clear of innumerable wars, tyrannies, and seditions, perished at last by this monster, as by a deadly disease. The people ate not only the herbs and roots that grew about the citadel, but sodden leather and oil bags, while he was indulging himself in riotous feasts and dancings in the daytime, or mimicking and laughing at the enemy. He let the sacred lamp of the goddess go out for want of oil; and when the principal priestess sent to ask him for half a measure of barley, he sent her that quantity of pepper.

An internal abscess compelled him to give up war. This abscess corrupted his flesh, so that, though he had many persons employed both day and night to clean him, his whole attire, his baths, his basins, and his food, were filled with a perpetual flux of vermin and corruption; and though he bathed many times a day, to cleanse and purify himself, it was in vain, and he died a terrible death.

Pompey conveyed the body to Rome, and conducted the whole funeral, not only with security, but with honor. Such was the quantity of spices brought in by the women that exclusive of those carried in two hundred and ten great baskets, a figure of Sylla at full length, and of a lictor besides, was made entirely of cinnamon and the choicest frankincense. The day happened to be so cloudy, and the rain was so much expected, that it was about three in the afternoon before the corpse was carried out. However, it was no sooner laid upon the pile than a brisk wind blew, and raised so strong a flame that it was consumed immediately. But after the pile was burnt down, and the fire began to die out, a great rain fell, which lasted till night, so that Sylla's good fortune continued to the last, and assisted at his funeral. His monument stands in the Campus Martius; and they tell us he wrote an epitaph for himself to this purport:—"No friend ever did me so much good, or enemy so much harm, but I repaid him with interest."

CIMON.

Note.—CIMON (Athenian). Cimon was born B.C. 519. His first memorable exploit was the capture of the important town of Eion on the Strymon, 476 B.C. Ten years later, he gained a great victory over the Persians. In B.C. 461, he was banished for ten years, but was recalled five years later. His death at the siege of Citium took place B.C. 449.

CIMON was the son of Miltiades and Hegesipyla. He was a person of no reputation, but censured as a disorderly and riotous young man. He was even compared to his grandfather Cimon, who, for his stupidity, was called Coalemus, that is, Idiot. He had no knowledge of music, or any other accomplishment which was in vogue among the Greeks, and he had not the least spark of the Attic wit or eloquence; but there was a generosity and sincerity in his behavior which showed the composition of his soul to be rather of the Peloponnesian kind. Like the Hercules of Euripides, he was

"Rough and unbred, but great on great occasions."

After several successful battles he had acquired a great fortune; and what he had gained gloriously in the war from the enemy, he laid out with as much reputation upon his fellow-citizens. He ordered the fences of his fields and gardens to be thrown down, that strangers, as well as his own countrymen, might freely partake of his fruit. He had a supper provided at his house every day, in which the dishes were plain, but sufficient for a multitude of guests. Every poor citizen repaired to it at pleasure, and had his diet without care or trouble; by which means he was enabled to give proper attention to public affairs.

When he walked out he used to have a retinue of young men, well clothed; and if he happened to meet an aged citizen in a mean dress, he ordered some one of them to change clothes with him. This was great and noble. But, besides this, the same attendants carried with them a quantity of money, and when they met in the market-place with any necessitous person of tolerable appearance, they took care to slip some pieces into his hand as privately as possible.

He was killed at the siege of Citium, and his remains were taken to Attica, where a monument bears the name Cimonia.

LUCULLUS.

Note.—LUCULLUS (Roman). Lucius Licinius Lucullus was born about B.C. 115. He was made consul B.C. 74 and was engaged with varying fortunes in the war against Mithridates for eight years. The enormous wealth which he brought from Asia enabled him to give magnificent feasts, build splendid gardens, parks and fish-ponds, and to indulge his luxurious tastes to the full. He died about B.C. 57.

THOUGH he was but a stripling at the time of the Marsian war, there appeared many instances of his courage and understanding; but Sylla's attachment to him was principally owing to his constancy and mildness. Amongst other things, he gave him the direction of the mint; and it was he who coined most of Sylla's money in Peloponnesus during the Mithridatic war. From him it was called Lucullia, and it continued to be chiefly in use for the army; for the goodness of it made it pass with ease.

During the time that he was Quæstor in Asia and Prætor in Africa, he rendered himself conspicuous by his justice and humanity. He was made consul, and had the conduct of the war against Mithridates. He was fortunate both by sea and land. He crossed the Euphrates and laid siege to Tigranocerta. The mixed multitude of barbarians in the city saw him, and in a menacing manner pointed to their king's armies before the walls.

Lucullus, before the battle, held a council of war. Some advised him to quit the siege and meet Tigranes with all his forces; others were of opinion that he should continue the siege, and not leave so many enemies behind him. He told them that neither separately gave good counsel, but both together did. He therefore divided his forces, and left Murena before the place with six thousand men; while he, with the rest of the infantry, consisting of twenty-four cohorts, which contained not more than ten thousand combatants, with all his cavalry, and about a thousand slingers and archers, marched against Tigranes, whose army was computed at two hundred thousand men. He encamped on a large plain with a river before him, where his army, appearing no more than a handful, afforded much matter of mirth to the flatterers of the king. Some ridiculed the diminutive appearance; others, by way of jest, cast lots for the spoil; and there was not one of the generals and princes who did not come and desire to be employed alone upon that service, while Tigranes needed only to sit still and look on. The king, too, thinking he must show himself facetious on the occasion, made use of that celebrated expression, "That if they came as ambassadors, there were too many of them; if as soldiers, too few." Thus they passed the first day in raillery. Next morning, at break of day, Lucullus drew out his army. The camp of the barbarians was on the east side of the river; but the river, where it is most fordable, makes a bend to the west. As Lucullus marched hastily down to that quarter, Tigranes thought he was retreating. Upon this, he called to Taxiles, and said with a scornful smile, "Seest thou not these invincible Roman legions taking to flight?" Taxiles answered, "I wish from my soul, my lord, that your good genius may work a miracle in your favor; but these legions do not use their best accouterments in a mere march. They do not wear their polished shields, nor take their bright helmets out of their cases, as you see they have now done. All this splendid appearance indicates their intention to fight, and to advance against their enemies as fast as possible." While Taxiles was yet speaking, they saw the eagle of the foremost legion make a motion to the right, by order of Lucullus, and the cohorts proceed in good order to pass the river. Then Tigranes, with much difficulty, awakened from his intoxication, and exclaimed two or three times, "Are these men coming against us?" After this, he drew out his forces in a hasty and disorderly manner, taking himself the command of the main body, and giving the left wing to the king of the Adiabenians, and the right to the king of the Medes. Before this right wing were placed most of the cavalry that were armed in steel.

As Lucullus was going to pass the river, some of his officers admonished him to beware of that day, which had been inauspicious, or, as they called it, a black one to the Romans; for on that day Cæpio's army was defeated by the Cimbri. Lucullus returned that memorable answer, "I will make this day, too, an auspicious one for Rome." It was the 6th of October. Having thus spoken, and withal exhorted his men to exert themselves, he advanced at the head of them against the enemy. He was armed with a breastplate of steel, formed in scales, which cast a surprising lustre; and the robe he wore over it was adorned with fringe. He drew his sword immediately, to show his troops the necessity of coming hand to hand with an enemy who were accustomed to fight at a distance, and by the vigor of their charge not to leave the enemy room to exercise their missive weapons. Observing that the enemy's heavy-armed cavalry, upon which they had their chief dependence, was covered by a hill that was plain and even at the top, and which, with an extent of only four furlongs, was not very difficult to ascend, he dispatched his Thracian and Gaulish horse with orders to take them on the flank, and to strike at nothing but the shafts of their pikes. Their whole strength, indeed, consists in the pike, and they have no other weapon, either offensive or defensive, that they can use, by reason of their heavy and unwieldy armor in which they are, as it were, immured.

Meanwhile he began to climb the hill with two companies of infantry, and the soldiers followed him with great readiness, when they saw him, encumbered as he was with his armor, the first to labor on foot up the ascent. When he had reached the summit, he stood on the most conspicuous part of it, and cried out, "The victory is ours, my fellow-soldiers, the victory is ours!" At the same time, he advanced against the heavy-armed cavalry, and ordered his men not to make any use of their javelins, but to come to close action, and to aim their blows at their enemies' legs and thighs, in which parts alone they were not armed. There was no need, however, to put this in execution; for, instead of standing to receive the Romans, the enemy set up a cry of fear, and most despicably fled, without striking a blow. In their flight they and their horses, heavy with armor, ran back upon their own infantry, and put them in confusion; insomuch that all those myriads were routed without standing to receive one wound, or spilling one drop of blood. Multitudes, however, were slain in their flight, or rather in their attempt to fly, their ranks being so thick and deep that they entangled and impeded each other.

Tigranes rode off, one of the first, with a few attendants; and seeing his son taking his share in his misfortune, he took the diadem from his head, gave it him, with tears, and desired him to save himself in the best manner he could by taking some other road. The young prince did not venture to wear it, but put it in the hands of one of his most faithful servants, who happened afterwards to be taken and brought to Lucullus; by this means the royal diadem of Tigranes added to the honors of the spoil. It is said that of the foot there fell above a hundred thousand, and of the horse very few escaped; whereas the Romans had but five killed, and a hundred wounded. Antiochus, the philosopher, in his Treatise concerning the Gods, speaking of this action, says the sun never beheld such another. Strabo, another philosopher, in his Historical Commentaries, informs us that the Romans were ashamed, and ridiculed each other for having employed weapons against such vile slaves. And Livy tells us, the Romans, with such inferior numbers, never engaged such a multitude as this. The victors did not, indeed, make up the twentieth part of the vanquished. The most able and experienced commanders among the Romans paid the highest compliments to the generalship of Lucullus, principally because he had defeated two of the greatest and most powerful kings in the world by methods entirely different; the one by an expeditious, and the other by a slow process.

Lucullus was a sumptuous liver, as the following particulars show. Crassus and Pompey ridiculed Lucullus for giving way to a life of pleasure and expense, thinking it full as unseasonable at his time of life to plunge into luxury, as to direct the administration or lead armies into the field. Among his frivolous amusements I cannot but reckon his sumptuous villas, walks, and baths, and still more, the paintings, statues, and other works of art, which he collected at an immense expense, idly squandering away upon them the vast fortune which he had amassed in the wars; insomuch, that even now, when luxury has made so much greater advances, the gardens of Lucullus are numbered with those of kings, and the most magnificent even of those. When Tubera, the Stoic, beheld his works on the sea-coast near Naples, the hills he had excavated for vaults and cellars, the reservoirs he had formed about his houses to receive the sea for the feeding of his fish, and his edifices in the sea itself, the philosopher called him Xerxes in a gown. Besides these, he had the most superb pleasure-houses in the country near Tusculum, adorned with grand galleries and open saloons, as well for the prospect as for walks. Pompey, on a visit there, blamed Lucullus for having made the villa commodious only for the summer, and absolutely uninhabitable in the winter. Lucullus answered with a smile, "What, then, do you think I have not so much sense as the cranes and storks, which change their habitations with the seasons?"

A prætor, who wanted to exhibit magnificent games, applied to Lucullus for some purple robes for the chorus in his tragedy; and he told him he would inquire whether he could furnish him or not. Next day he asked him how many he wanted. The prætor answered, "A hundred would be sufficient;" upon which Lucullus said, "He might have twice that number if he pleased." The poet Horace makes this remark on the occasion:—

> " Poor is the house where plenty has not stores
> That miss the master's eye——"

His daily repasts were like those of a man suddenly grown rich; pompous not only in the beds, which were covered with purple carpets, the sideboards of plate set with precious stones, and all the entertainment which musicians and comedians could furnish; but in the vast variety and exquisite dressing of the provisions. These things excited the admiration of men of unenlarged minds. Pompey, therefore, was highly applauded for the answer he gave his physician in a fit of sickness. The physician had ordered him to eat a thrush, and his servants told him, "That, as it was summer, there were no thrushes to be found, except in the aviaries of Lucullus." But he would not suffer them to apply for them there, and said to his physician, "Must Pompey then have died, if Lucullus had not been an epicure?"

The great expense he incurred in collecting

books deserves approbation. The number of volumes was great, and they were written in elegant hands; yet the use he made of them was more honorable than the acquisition. His libraries were open to all. The Greeks repaired at pleasure to the galleries and porticos, as to the retreat of the Muses, and there spent whole days in conversation on matters of learning—delighted to retire to such a scene from business and from care. Lucullus himself often joined these learned men in their walks, and conferred with them, and when he was applied to about the affairs of their country he gave them his assistance and advice; so that his house was in fact an asylum and senate house to all the Greeks who visited Rome.

Lucullus bestowed the time which was not employed in war on the promotion of law and justice. These had long lost their influence in Asia, which was then overwhelmed with unspeakable misfortunes. It was desolated and enslaved by the farmers of the revenue, and by usurers. The poor inhabitants were forced to sell the most beautiful of their sons and daughters, the ornaments and offerings in their temples, their paintings, and the statues of their gods. The last resource was to serve their creditors as slaves. Their sufferings prior to this were more cruel and insupportable; prisons, racks, tortures, exposures to the burning sun in summer, and in winter to the extremity of cold, amidst ice or mire; insomuch that servitude seemed a happy deliverance. Lucullus, finding the cities in such dreadful distress, soon rescued the oppressed from all their burdens. In the first place, he ordered the creditors not to take above one per centum for a month's interest; in the next place, he abolished all interest that exceeded the principal; the third and most important regulation was, that the creditor should not take above a fourth part of the debtor's income; and if any one took interest upon interest, he was to lose all. By these means, in less than four years, all the debts were paid, and the estates restored free to the proprietors. Lucullus died in the fifty-eighth year of his age, greatly regretted by the people.

NICIAS.

Note.—NICIAS (Athenian). Caution was the leading characteristic of this general, who played a prominent part in the Peloponnesian war. He negotiated the Peace of Nicias, 421 B.C., by which the Athenians and Spartans agreed to a truce for fifteen years. In many respects this brave general was the special target of misfortune.

THIS Athenian general was celebrated for his valor and for his misfortunes. He took Cythera, an island well situated for annoying Laconia, and at that time inhabited by Lacedæmonians. He recovered many places in Thrace, which had revolted from the Athenians. He shut up the Megarensians within their walls, and reduced the island of Minoa. From thence he made an excursion soon after, and got possession of the port of Nisæa. He likewise made a descent upon the territories of Corinth, beat the troops of that state in a pitched battle, and killed great numbers of them; Lycophron, their general, being among the slain.

He happened to leave there the bodies of two of his men, who were missed in carrying off the dead. But as soon as he knew it he stopped his course, and sent a herald to the enemy to ask leave to take away those bodies. This he did, though there was a law and custom existing by which those who desire a treaty for carrying off the dead give up the victory, and are not at liberty to erect a trophy. And indeed, those who are so far masters of the field that the enemy cannot bury their dead without permission, appear to be conquerors, because no man would ask as a favor that which he could command. Nicias, however, chose rather to lose his laurels than to leave two of his countrymen unburied.

One of the failings of Nicias was laziness, as we may read in Aristophanes' comedy of "'The Birds," where he says, "By heaven! this is no time for us to slumber, or to imitate the lazy operations of Nicias."

At the siege of Syracuse Lucullus was in chief command, and that place would have surrendered to him had not the sudden appearance of Gylippus, the Corinthian, an ally of the Sicilians, given them courage at the critical moment. Gylippus proposed terms of peace, but the Athenians refused them; and after some battles, in which Nicias was defeated, Demosthenes was sent with a powerful fleet to assist him. Over-eagerness, however, was the cause of the defeat of Demosthenes. This was a severe blow to Nicias, though it was what he expected; and he inveighed against the rash proceedings of Demosthenes. That general defended himself as well as he could, but at the same time gave it as his opinion that they should embark and return home as fast as possible. "We cannot hope," said he, "either for another army, or to conquer with the forces we have. Nay, supposing we had the advantage, we ought to relinquish a situation which is well known at all times to be unhealthy for the troops, and which now we find still more fatal from the season of the year."

Demosthenes urged the matter no further, because his former counsels had proved unfortunate. But as fresh forces came to the assistance of the Syracusans, and the sickness prevailed more and more in the Athenian camp, Nicias ordered the troops to be ready to embark. Everything was accordingly prepared for embarkation, but in the night there happened an eclipse of the moon, in which Nicias and all the rest of his warriors were struck with a great panic, looking upon the phenomenon as a bad omen. It was a great unhappiness to Nicias that he had not then with him an able diviner. Stilbides, whom he employed on such occasions, and who used to lessen the influence of his superstition, died a little before. Supposing the eclipse a portent, it could not, as Philochorus observes, be inauspicious to those who wanted to fly, but, on the contrary,

very favorable. For whatever is transacted with
fear seeks the shades of darkness: light is the
worst enemy. Besides, on other occasions, as
Auticlides remarks in his Commentaries, there
were only three days that people refrained from
business after an eclipse of either sun or moon;
whereas Nicias wanted to stay another entire revolution of the moon, as if he could not see her as
bright as ever the moment she passed the shadow
caused by the interposition of the earth.

But while he was waiting for more favorable
prognostications the Syracusans surrounded him
and attacked him by sea and land, and utterly defeated him. Demosthenes was taken prisoner,
and the troops he had the conduct of were surrounded. Upon hearing this Nicias begged to
treat with Gylippus, and offered hostages for paying the Syracusans the whole charge of the war,
on condition they would suffer the Athenians to
quit Sicily. The Syracusans rejected the proposal with every mark of insolence and outrage,
and fell again upon the wretched man, who was
in want of all manner of necessaries. He defended himself, however, all that night and continued his march the next day to the river Asi-
naarus. The enemy galled his troops all the way,
and when they came to the banks of the river
pushed them in. Nay, some of them, impatient to
quench their burning thirst, voluntarily plunged
into the stream. Then followed a most cruel
scene of blood and slaughter, the poor wretches
being massacred as they were drinking. At last

Nicias threw himself at the feet of Gylippus, and said, "Gylippus, you should show some compassion amidst your victory. I ask nothing for myself. What is life to a man whose misfortunes are even proverbial? But with respect to the other Athenians, methinks you should remember that the chance of war is uncertain, and with what humanity and moderation they treated you when they were victorious."

Gylippus was somewhat affected both at the sight of Nicias and at his speech. He knew the good offices he had done the Lacedæmonians at the last treaty of peace, and he was sensible it would contribute greatly to his honor if he could take two of the enemy's generals prisoners. Therefore, raising Nicias from the ground, he bade him take courage, and gave orders that the other Athenians should have quarter. But as the order was slowly communicated, the number of those that were saved were greatly inferior to that of the slain, though the soldiers spared several unknown to their officers.

The Athenians did not at first give credit to the news of this misfortune, the person who bore it not appearing to deserve their notice. It seems, a stranger who landed in the Piræus, as he sat to be shaved in a barber's shop, spoke of it as of an event already known to the Athenians. The barber no sooner heard it than he ran into the city, and informed the magistrates of the news in open court. Trouble and dismay seized all that heard it. The magistrates immediately summoned an assembly, and introduced the informant. There he was interrogated of whom he had the intelligence; and as he could give no clear and pertinent answer, he was considered as a forger of false news and a public incendiary. In this light he was fastened to the wheel, where he bore the torture for some time, till at length some credible persons arrived, who gave a distinct account of the whole disaster.

Nicias, and his general Demosthenes, were put to death by the Syracusans B.C. 413.

MARCUS CRASSUS.

Note.—MARCUS CRASSUS (Roman). This immensely rich consul and triumvir defeated the insurgent gladiators, B.C. 71. He and Pompey were personal enemies, but Cæsar brought about a reconciliation, B.C. 60, when the first triumvir was formed. The legend is that after Crassus was slain in battle, Orodes, king of Parthia, had melted gold poured into the dead man's mouth, with the taunt : " Sate thyself now with that metal of which in life thou wert so greedy."

CRASSUS had but one vice, which cast a shade upon his many virtues, namely, avarice. He made money in many ways. He had observed how liable the city was to fires, and how frequently houses fell down owing to the weight of the buildings, and their standing so close together. In consequence of this he provided himself with slaves who were carpenters and masons, and went on collecting them till he had upwards of five hundred. Then he made it his business to buy houses that were on fire, and others that joined them, and he commonly had them at a low price by reason of the fear and distress the owners were in about the fire. Hence in time he became master of great part of Rome. But though he had so many workmen, he built no more for himself than one house in which he lived; for he used to say, "That those who love building will soon ruin themselves, and need no other enemies."

Though he had several silver mines and lands of great value, the revenue he drew from them was nothing in comparison with that produced by his slaves; such a number had he of them, and all useful in life,—readers, amanuenses, bookkeepers, stewards, and cooks. He used to attend to their education, and often gave them lessons himself; esteeming it a principal part of the business of a master to inspect and take care of his servants, whom he considered as the living instruments of economy. In this he was certainly right, if he thought, as he often said, that other matters should be managed by servants, but the servants by the master. He was wrong, however, in saying that no man ought to be esteemed rich who could not with his own revenue maintain an army; for, as Archidamus observes, it never can be calculated what such a monster as war will devour.

Crassus behaved in a generous manner to strangers; his house was always open to them; and he used to lend money to his friends without interest. Nevertheless, his rigor in demanding his money the very day it was due often made his apparent favor a greater inconvenience than the paying of interest would have been. As to his invitations, they were most of them to the commonalty; and though there was a simplicity in the provision, yet at the same time there was a neatness and unceremonious welcome, which made it more agreeable than more expensive tables.

As to his studies, he cultivated oratory—most particularly that of the bar, which had its superior utility. And though he might, upon the whole, be reckoned equal to the first-rate speakers, yet by his care and application he exceeded those whom nature had favored more; for there was not a cause, however unimportant, to which he did not come prepared. Besides, when Pompey and Cæsar and Cicero refused to speak, he often rose and finished the argument in favor of the defendant. This attention of his to assist any unfortunate citizen made him very popular, and his obliging manner in his common address had an equal charm. There was not a Roman, however mean and insignificant, whom he did not salute, or whose salutation he did not return by name.

Rome was at this time divided into three parties, at the head of which were Pompey, Cæsar, and Crassus; for as to Cato, his reputation was greater than his power, and his virtue more admired than followed. The prudent and steady part of the city were for Pompey; the violent and the enterprising gave in to the prospects of Cæsar; Crassus steered a middle course, and availed himself of both. Crassus, indeed, often changed sides, and neither was a firm friend nor an implacable enemy. On the contrary, he frequently gave up either his attachments or resentments indifferently when his interest required it; insomuch that in a short space of time he would appear either in support or opposition to the same persons and laws.

As a soldier, Crassus was at first successful; but he was betrayed into the hands of Surena, a general of the forces of Orodes, King of Parthia, and was put to death B.C. 53. A poet of the period says that he was

"In all trades skilled except the trade of war."

SERTORIUS.

Note.—SERTORIUS (Roman). This distinguished Roman general was made quæstor, B.C. 91. He commanded the Cinnæ at the siege of Rome, B.C. 87. His despotic acts weakened his influence and popularity and brought about his assassination as narrated by Plutarch.

QUINTUS SERTORIUS was of a respectable family in the town of Nursia and country of the Sabines. Having lost his father when a child, he had a liberal education given him by his mother, Rhea, whom on that account he always loved with the greatest tenderness. He was sufficiently qualified to speak in a court of justice, and by his abilities that way gained some interest in Rome itself when but a youth. But his greater talents for the camp, and his success as a soldier, turned his ambition into that channel.

He made his first campaign under Cæpio, when the Cimbri and Teutones broke into Gaul. The Romans fought a battle, in which their behavior was but indifferent, and they were put to the rout. On this occasion Sertorius lost his horse, and received many wounds himself, yet he swam the river Rhone, armed as he was with his breastplate and shield, in spite of the violence of the torrent, —such was his strength of body, and so much had he improved that strength by exercise. The same enemy came on a second time, in such prodigious numbers and with dreadful menaces that it was difficult to prevail with a Roman to keep his post, or to obey his general. Marius had then the command, and Sertorius offered his service to go as a spy, and bring him an account of the enemy. For this purpose he took a Gaulish habit, and having learned as much of the language as might suffice for common address, he mingled with the barbarians. When he had seen and heard enough to let him into the measures they were taking, he returned to Marius, who honored him with the established rewards of valor; and during that whole war he gave such proofs of his courage and capacity as raised him to distinction, and perfectly gained him the confidence of his general.

The Characitani are seated beyond the river Tagus. They have neither cities nor villages, but dwell upon a large and lofty hill, in dens and caverns of the rocks, the mouths of which are all to the north. The soil of all the country about it is a clay so very light and crumbly that it yields to the pressure of the foot, is reduced to powder with the least touch, and flies about like ashes or unslaked lime. The barbarians, whenever they are apprehensive of an attack, retire to these caves with their booty, and look upon themselves as in a place perfectly impregnable.

It happened that Sertorius, retiring to some distance from Metellus, encamped under this hill; and the savage inhabitants, imagining he retired only because he was beaten, offered him several insults. Sertorius, either provoked at such treatment, or willing to show them he was not flying from any enemy, mounted his horse the next day, and went to reconnoiter the place. As he could see no part in which it was accessible, he almost despaired of taking it, and could only vent his anger in vain menaces. At last he observed that the wind blew the dust in great quantities toward the mouths of the caves, which, as I said before, are all to the north. The north wind, which some call "cæcias," prevails most in those parts, and as it was then the height of summer, it was remarkably strong. Sertorius, reflecting upon what he saw, and being informed by the neighboring Spaniards that these were the usual appearances, ordered his soldiers to collect vast quantities of that dry and crumbly earth, so as to raise a mound of it over against the hill. The barbarians, imagining he intended to storm their strongholds from that mound, laughed at his proceedings. The soldiers went on with their work till night, and then he led them back into the camp. Next morning, at break of day, a gentle breeze sprang up, which moved the lightest part of the heap, and dispersed it like smoke; and as the sun got up higher, the "cæcias" blew again, and by its violence covered all the hill with dust. Meantime the soldiers stirred up the heap from the very bottom, and crumbled all the clay; and some galloped up and down to raise the light earth, and thicken the clouds of dust in the wind, which carried them into the dwellings of the Characitani, their entrances directly facing it. As they were caves, and of course had no other opening, the eyes of the inhabitants were soon filled, and they could scarce breathe for the suffocating dust which they drew in with the air. In these wretched circumstances they held out two days, though with great difficulty, and the third day surrendered themselves to Sertorius at discretion, who, by reducing them, did not gain such an accession of strength as of honor; for an honor it was to subdue those by stratagem whom his arms could not reach.

After a time, one of his officers became jealous of his general's fame, and formed a conspiracy to kill him at an entertainment. The entertainments at which Sertorius was present had been always attended with great order and decorum; for he could not bear either to see or hear the least indecency, and he had ever accustomed the guests to divert themselves in an innocent and irreproachable manner. But in the midst of the entertainment the conspirators began to seek occasion to quarrel, introduced the most dissolute discourse, and pretending drunkenness as the cause of their ribaldry. All this was done to provoke him. However, either vexed at their obscenities and discourses, or guessing at their design, he changed his posture, and threw himself back upon his couch, as though he neither heard nor regarded them. Then Perpenna took a cup of wine, and as he was drinking purposely let it fall out of his hands. The noise it made being the signal for them to fall on, Antony, who sat next to Sertorius, gave him a stroke with his sword. Sertorius turned, and strove to get up; but Antony, throwing himself upon his breast, held both his hands: so that, not being able in the least to defend himself, the other conspirators dispatched him with many wounds.

This happened B.C. 72.

EUMENES.

Note.—EUMENES (Greek). Eumenes was accounted the most worthy of all the officers of Alexander the Great to succeed him after his death. His career is fully told in the sketch. He was born 360 B.C.

THIS Grecian general was the son of a poor wagoner, but he was well educated, and practiced the exercises in vogue at those times. While he was but a lad, Philip, who happened to be in Cardia, went to see how the young men acquitted themselves at the boxing and wrestling. Eumenes got on so well, and showed so much activity, that Philip was pleased with him and took him into his train. After Philip's death he maintained the reputation of being equal to any of Alexander's officers. His hand-to-hand fight with Neoptolemus made him famous. A most violent hatred had long subsisted between them, and this day added stings to it. They rushed forward impetuously with swords drawn, and loud shouts. The shock their horses met with was so violent that it resembled that of two galleys. The fierce antagonists quitted the bridles, and laid hold on each other, each endeavoring to tear off the helmet or the breastplate of his enemy. While their hands were thus engaged their horses went from under them, and as they fell to the ground, without quitting their hold, they wrestled for the advantage. Neoptolemus was beginning to rise first, when Eumenes wounded him in the ham, and by that means got upon his feet before him. Neoptolemus being wounded in one knee supported himself upon the other, and fought with great courage underneath, but was not able to give his adversary a mortal blow. At last, receiving a wound in the neck, he grew faint, and stretched himself upon the ground. Eumenes, with all the eagerness of inveterate hatred, hastening to strip him of his arms, and loading him with reproaches, did not observe that his sword was still in his hand; so that Neoptolemus wounded him under the cuirass where it touches upon the groin. However, as the stroke was but feeble, the apprehensions it gave him were greater than the real hurt.

On one occasion when there was a conspiracy to kill him he pretended that he was in want of money, and borrowed large sums of those that hated him most, in order that they might give up their designs upon his life out of regard to the money lent him. Thus he found guards for himself in the opulence of others; and though men in general seek to save their lives by giving, he provided for his safety by borrowing.

It was agreed to make use of him in the ensuing battle, and to assassinate him immediately after. But Eudamus, master of the elephants, and Phædimus, privately informed Eumenes of the resolutions, not out of any kindness or benevolent regard, but because they were afraid of losing the money they had lent him. He commended them for the honor with which they behaved, and retired to his tent. There he told his friends, "That he lived among a herd of savage beasts," and immediately made his will. After which he destroyed all his papers, lest, after his death, charges and impeachments should arise against the persons who wrote them, in consequence of the secrets discovered therein. Thus foiled, these conspirators betrayed him into the hands of Antigonus at Nora, in Cappadocia, and he was killed B.C. 315.

AGESILAUS.

Note.—AGESILAUS (Greek). The career of Agesilaus was a glorious one. He was past four-score, and had reigned more than forty years, as king of Lacedæmon, when returning from his campaign in Egypt, he was wrecked off the coast of Libya and perished B.C. 360.

ARCHIDAMUS II., King of Sparta, left two sons, Agis and Agesilaus, and as the crown by law was to descend to Agis, Agesilaus only had the education of a private citizen, which, though hard in respect of diet, and full of laborious exercises, was well calculated to teach obedience and submission to the laws. He was lame of one leg; but that defect, during his youth, was covered by the agreeable turn of the rest of his person, and his easy and cheerful manner. He would not suffer any portrait or statue of him to be made while he lived, and at his death he utterly forbade it. We are only told that he was a little man, and that he had not a commanding aspect. But a perpetual vivacity and cheerfulness, attended with a talent for raillery, which was expressed without any severity either of voice or look, made him more agreeable, even in age, than the young and the handsome. Theophrastus tells us, the ephori fined Archidamus for marrying a little woman. "She will bring us," said they, "a race of pigmies instead of kings."

Agis died young, and Agesilaus then gained the diadem, and was at the same time put in possession of his brother's private estate. He was very successful as a soldier till sickness compelled his retirement, and it is universally agreed that he saved Sparta by controlling his native passions of obstinacy and ambition, and pursuing no measures but what were safe. He could not, indeed, restore the city to her former glory and power. The constitution was admirably formed for peace, for virtue, and harmony; but when they wanted to add to their dominions by force of arms, and to make acquisitions which Lycurgus thought unnecessary to their happiness, they split upon that rock he had warned them to avoid.

Agesilaus now declined the service on account of his great age. He died in Africa at the age of eighty-four, of which he had reigned forty-one in Lacedæmon. During thirty years of that time he made the greatest figure, both as to reputation and power, being looked upon as commander-in-chief, and, as it were, king of Greece, till the battle of Leuctra.

It was the custom of the Spartans to bury persons of ordinary rank in the place where they expired, when they happened to die, as Agesilaus did, in a foreign country, but to carry the corpses of the kings home: and as the attendants of Agesilaus had not honey to preserve the body, they embalmed it with melted wax, and so conveyed it to Lacedæmon.

POMPEY.

Note.—POMPEY (Roman). Pompey was born 106 B.C. A full account of his remarkable life and career is given in the sketch which follows. His treacherous assassination in Egypt took place B.C. 48. His head was cut off and sent to Cæsar, who shed tears and turned away at the sight.

IN his youth Pompey had a very engaging countenance, which spoke for him before he opened his lips. Yet that grace of aspect was not unattended with dignity, and amidst his youthful bloom there was a venerable and princely air. His hair curled a little naturally in front, which, together with the shining moisture and quick turn of his eye, produced a strong likeness of Alexander the Great.

Having made considerable progress in the military art, he pleased Sylla, but could not persuade him to grant him (Pompey) a triumph for his victories. Pompey resented this, and the people supported him. When Sylla heard that Pompey had revolted, he said to his friends, "Then it is my fate to have to contend with boys in my old age." When he observed that all the people flocked out to receive Pompey, and to conduct him home with marks of great regard, he resolved to exceed them in his regards if possible. He therefore hastened to meet him, and, embracing him in the most affectionate manner, saluted him aloud by the surname of Magnus, or The Great. At the same time he ordered all about him to give him the same appellation. In this respect we may justly admire the wisdom of the ancient Romans, who bestowed on their great men such honorable names and titles, not only for military achievements, but for the great qualities and arts which adorn civil life.

Yet when Crassus was elected consul they disagreed in everything and were embroiled in all their measures. Crassus had most interest with the senate, and Pompey with the people. The most agreeable spectacle to the people was Pompey himself, when he went to claim his exemption from serving in the wars. It was the custom for a Roman knight, when he had served the time ordered by law, to lead his horse into the forum before the two magistrates called censors, and, after having given account of the generals and other officers under whom he had made his campaigns, and of his own actions in them, to demand his discharge. On these occasions they received proper marks of honor or disgrace, according to their behavior.

When the censors had taken their seats to review the whole equestrian order, Pompey was seen at a distance, with all the badges of his office as consul, leading his horse by the bridle. As soon as he was near enough to be observed by the censors he ordered his lictors to make an opening, and advanced with his horse in hand to the foot of the tribunal. The people were struck with admiration, and a profound silence ensued; at the same time, a joy, mingled with reverence, was visible in the countenance of the censors. The senior censor then addressed him as follows: "Pompey the Great, I demand of you whether you have served all the campaigns required by law!" He answered with a loud voice, "I have served them all, and all under myself as general." The people were so charmed with this answer that there seemed no end to their acclamations.

About this time the pirates had become very troublesome. The Romans being engaged in civil wars at the very gates of their capital, the sea was left unguarded. The pirates not only attacked ships, but islands and maritime towns. Many persons distinguished for their wealth, their birth, and their capacity, embarked with them, and assisted in their depredations, as if their employment had been worthy the ambition of men of honor. They had in various places arsenals, ports, and watch-towers, all strongly fortified. Their fleets were not only extremely well-manned, supplied with skilful pilots, and fitted for their business by their lightness and celerity, but there was a parade of vanity about them more mortifying than their strength, in gilded sterns, purple canopies, and plated oars, as if they took a pride in their villainy. Music resounded and drunken revels were exhibited on every coast. Here generals were made prisoners; there the cities the pirates had taken were paying their ransom, all to the great disgrace of the Roman power. The number of their galleys amounted to a thousand, and they were masters of four hundred cities.

Their power extended over the whole Tuscan Sea, so that the Romans found their trade and navigation entirely cut off; the consequence of which was that their markets were not supplied, and they had reason to apprehend a famine. This at last suggested their sending Pompey to clear the sea of pirates. In pursuance of his charge he divided the whole Mediterranean into thirteen parts, appointing a lieutenant for each, and assigning him a squadron. By thus stationing his fleets in all quarters, he inclosed the pirates, as it were, in a net, took great numbers of them, and brought them into harbor. Such of their vessels as had dispersed and made off in time, or could escape the general chase, retired to Cilicia, like so many bees into a hive. Against these he proposed to go himself with sixty of his best galleys; but first he resolved to clear the Tuscan Sea, and the coasts of Africa, Sardinia, Corsica, and Sicily, of all piratical adventurers, which he effected in forty days.

As soon as the people were informed of his return to Rome they went in crowds to receive him, in the same manner as they had done a few days before, to conduct him on his way. Their extraordinary joy was owing to the speed with which he had executed his commission, so far beyond all expectation, and to the superabundant plenty which reigned in the markets.

He was passionately desirous to recover Syria, and passing from thence through Arabia, to penetrate to the Red Sea, that he might go on conquering every way to the ocean which surrounds the world. In Africa he was the first whose conquests extended to the Great Sea; in Spain he stretched the Roman dominions to the Atlantic; and in his late pursuit of the Albanians he wanted but little of reaching the Hyrcanian Sea. In order, therefore, to take the Red Sea too into the circle of his wars, he began his march, the rather because he saw it difficult to hunt out Mithridates with a regular force, and that he was much harder to deal with in his flight than in battle. For this reason he said, "He would leave him a stronger enemy than the Romans to cope with, which was famine." In pursuance of this intention he ordered a number of ships to cruise about and prevent any vessels from entering the Bosphorus with provisions, and that death should be the punishment for such as were taken in the attempt.

Proceeding in the execution of his plan, he subdued the Arabians about Mount Amanus by his lieutenant Afranius, and descended himself into Syria, which he converted into a Roman province, because it had no lawful king. He reduced Judea, and took its king Aristobulus prisoner. He founded some cities and set others free, punishing the tyrants who had enslaved them; but most of his time was spent in administering justice, and in deciding the disputes between cities and princes.

Pompey having thus brought the campaign and the whole war to a conclusion so happy, and so far beyond his hopes, immediately quitted Arabia, traversed the provinces between that and Galatia with great rapidity, and soon arrived at Amisus. There he found many presents from Pharnaces, and several corpses of the royal family, among which was that of Mithridates. The face of that prince could not be easily known, because the embalmers had not taken out the brain, and by the corruption of that the features were disfigured. As for Pompey, he would not see the body, but, to propitiate the avenging deity, sent it to Sinope. However, he looked upon and admired the magnificence of his habit and the size and beauty of his weapons.

The triumph was so great that, though it was divided into two days, the time was far from being sufficient for displaying what was prepared to be carried in procession,—there remained still enough to adorn another triumph. At the head of the show appeared the titles of the conquered nations, —Pontus, Armenia, Cappadocia, Paphlagonia, Media, Colchis, the Iberians, the Albanians, Syria, Cilicia, Mesopotamia, Phœnicia, Palestine, Judea, and Arabia, and the pirates subdued both by sea and land. In these countries it was mentioned that there were not less than a thousand castles and near nine hundred cities taken, eight hundred galleys taken from the pirates, and thirty-nine desolate cities repeopled. On the face of the tablets it appeared besides, that whereas the revenues of the Roman Empire before these conquests amounted but to fifty millions of drachmas, by the new acquisitions they were advanced to eighty-five millions; and that Pompey had brought into the public treasury in money, and in gold and silver vessels, to the value of twenty thousand talents, besides what he had distributed among the soldiers, of whom he that received least had fifteen hundred drachmas to his share. The captives who walked in the procession (not to mention the chiefs of the pirates) were—the son of Tigranes, King of Armenia, together with his wife and daughter; Zosima, the wife of Tigranes himself; Aristobulus, King of Judea; the sister of Mithridates, with her five sons; and some Scythian women. The hostages of the Albanians and Iberians, and of the King of Commagene, also appeared in the train.

But the most honorable circumstance, and what no other Roman could boast, was that his first triumph was over Africa, his second over Europe, and his third over Asia; so that the three seemed to declare him conqueror over the world.

In the meantime the wars in Gaul lifted Cæsar to the first sphere of greatness. The scene of action was at a great distance from Rome, and he seemed to be wholly engaged with the Belgæ, the Suevi, and the Britons; but his genius all the while was privately at work among the people of Rome, and he was undermining Pompey in his most essential interests. The gold and silver and other rich spoils which he took from the enemy in great abundance he sent to Rome, and by distributing them freely among the ædiles, prætors, consuls, and their wives, he gained a great party.

Consequently, when he passed the Alps and wintered at Lucca, among the crowd of men and women who hastened to pay their respects to him there were two hundred senators, Pompey and Crassus of the number. Cæsar entered into a treaty with Crassus and Pompey, by which it was agreed that they should apply for the consulship, and that he should assist them by sending a great number of his soldiers to vote at the election. As soon as they were chosen they were to share the provinces and take the command of armies according to their pleasure, only confirming Cæsar in the possession of what he had for five years more.

Crassus, upon the expiration of his consulship, repaired to his province. Pompey, remaining at Rome, opened his theater, and, to make the dedication more magnificent, exhibited a variety of gymnastic games, entertainments of music, and battles with wild beasts, in which were killed five hundred lions ; but the battle of elephants afforded the most astonishing spectacle.

Pompey then went into the city and married Cornelia, the daughter of Metellus Scipio. She was a widow, having been married when very young to Publius, the son of Crassus, who was lately killed in the Parthian expedition. This woman had many charms beside her beauty. She was well versed in polite literature ; she played upon the lyre, and understood geometry ; and she had made considerable improvements by the precepts of philosophy. What is more, she had nothing of that petulance and affectation which such studies are apt to produce in women of her age.

Being again elected consul, his first step was to bring those to account who had gained offices and employments by bribery and corruption, and he made laws by which the proceedings in their trials were to be regulated. He behaved with great dignity and honor, and restored security, order, and tranquillity to the courts of judicature by presiding there in person with a band of soldiers. But when Scipio, his father-in-law, came to be impeached, he sent for the three hundred and sixty judges to his house and desired their assistance. The accuser, seeing Scipio conducted out of the forum to his house by the judges themselves, dropped the prosecution. This again exposed Pompey to censure; but he was censured still more when, after having made a law against encomiums on persons accused, he broke it himself by appearing for Plancus, and attempting to embellish his character. Cato, who happened to be one of the judges, stopped his ears, declaring, "It was not right for him to hear such embellishments contrary to the law." Cato, therefore, was objected to and set aside before sentence was passed. Plancus, however, was condemned by the other judges, to the great confusion of Pompey.

The rupture between Cæsar and Pompey was now complete, but the latter expressed no fear; and when the citizens said that if Cæsar should advance on Rome in a hostile manner they did not see what forces they had to oppose him, Pompey, with a smile, bade them give themselves no concern, for, said he, "If in Italy I do but stamp upon the ground an army will appear."

Cæsar, however, was exerting himself greatly; and the quarrel having come before the senate, Marcellus, the consul, called Cæsar a public robber, and insisted that he should be declared an enemy to the State if he did not lay down his arms. However, Curio, together with Antony and Piso, prevailed that a further inquiry should be made into the sense of the senate. He first proposed that such as were of opinion "that Cæsar should disband his army and Pompey keep his," should draw to one side of the house; and there appeared a majority for that motion. Then he proposed that the number of those should be taken whose sense it was "that both should lay down their arms, and neither remain in command;" upon which question Pompey had only twenty-two, and Curio all the rest. Curio, proud of his victory, ran in transports of joy to the assembly of the people, who received him with the loudest plaudits, and crowned him with flowers. Pompey was not present at the debate in the house; for the commander of an army is not allowed to enter the city. But Marcellus rose up and said, "I will no longer sit to hear the matter canvassed; but, as I see ten legions have already passed the Alps, I will send a man to oppose them in behalf of my country."

At the same time news was brought that Cæsar

had seized Ariminum, a considerable city in Italy, and that he was marching directly toward Rome with all his forces. The last circumstance, indeed, was not true. He advanced with only three hundred horse and five thousand foot; the rest of his forces were on the other side the Alps and he would not wait for them, choosing rather to put his adversaries in confusion by a sudden and unexpected attack, than to fight them when better prepared. When he came to the river Rubicon, which was the boundary of his province, he stood silent a long time, weighing with himself the greatness of his enterprise. At last, like one who plunges down from the top of a precipice into a gulf of immense depth, he silenced his reason, and shut his eyes against the danger, and crying out, "The die is cast," he marched over with his army.

Upon the first report of this at Rome the city was in greater disorder and astonishment than had ever been known. The senate and the magistrates ran immediately to Pompey. Tullus asked him what forces he had ready for the war, and as he hesitated in his answer, and only said at last, in a tone of no great assurance, "That he had the two legions lately sent him back by Cæsar, and that out of the new levies he believed he should shortly be able to make up a body of thirty thousand men," Tullus exclaimed, "O Pompey, you have deceived us!" and gave it as his opinion that ambassadors should immediately be dispatched to Cæsar. Then one Favonius, a man otherwise of no ill character, but who, by an insolent brutality, affected to imitate the noble freedom of Cato, bade Pompey "stamp upon the ground, and call for the armies he had promised."

Cato then advised that Pompey should not only be appointed general, but invested with a discretionary power, adding, "That those who were the authors of great evils knew best how to cure them." Pompey, at last, as he could get no certain intelligence of Cæsar's motions, caused an edict to be issued declaring the commonwealth in danger and no peace to be expected. He told those who wished to remain in the city that he should consider them as partisans of Cæsar, and he and the consuls all fled.

A few days after Cæsar arrived at Rome. When he was in possession of the city he behaved with great moderation, and composed in a good measure the minds of its remaining inhabitants. Only when Metellus, one of the tribunes of the people, forbade him to touch the money in the public treasury, he threatened him with death, adding an expression more terrible than the threat itself, "That it was easier for him to *do* it than to *say* it." Metellus being thus frightened off, Cæsar took what sums he wanted, and then went in pursuit of Pompey, hastening to drive him out of Italy before his forces could arrive from Spain.

Pompey, who was master of Brundusium, and had a sufficient number of transports, desired the consuls to embark without loss of time, and sent them before him with thirty cohorts to Dyrrhachium. At the same time he sent his father-in-law, Scipio, and his son, Cnæus, into Syria to provide ships of war. He had well secured the gates of the city, and planted the lightest of his slingers and archers upon the walls; and having now ordered the Brundusians to keep within doors, he caused a number of trenches to be cut, and sharp stakes to be driven into them, and then covered with earth, in all the streets except two which led down to the sea. In three days all his other troops were embarked without interruption, and then he suddenly gave the signal to those who guarded the walls, in consequence of which they ran swiftly down to the harbor and got on board. Thus, having his whole complement, he set sail and crossed the sea to Dyrrhachium.

When Cæsar came and saw the walls left destitute of defense he concluded that Pompey had taken to flight, and in his eagerness to pursue would certainly have fallen upon the sharp stakes in the trenches, had not the Brundusians informed him of them. He then avoided the streets and took a circuit round the town, by which he discovered that all the vessels were set out except two that had not many soldiers aboard.

This manœuver of Pompey was commonly reckoned among his greatest acts of generalship. Cæsar having thus made himself master of all Italy in sixty days without the least bloodshed, marched to Spain with the intention of gaining forces there. This he did, and incorporated the troops with his own.

In the meantime Pompey assembled a great army, and at sea he was altogether invincible; for he had five hundred ships of war, and the number of his lighter vessels was still greater. As for his land forces, he had seven thousand horse, the flower of Rome and Italy, all men of family, fortune, and courage. His infantry, though numerous, was a mixture of raw undisciplined soldiers. He therefore exercised them during his stay at Berœa, where he was by no means idle, but went through all the exercises of a soldier as if he had been in the flower of his age. It inspired his troops with new courage when they saw Pompey the Great, at the age of fifty-eight, going through the whole military discipline in heavy armor on foot, and then mounting his horse, drawing his sword with ease when at full speed, and as dexterously sheathing it again. As to the javelin, he threw it not only with great exactness, but with such force that few of the young men could dart it to a greater distance.

Many kings and princes repaired to his camp, and the number of Roman officers who had commanded armies was so great that it was sufficient to make up a complete senate. Labienus, who had been honored with Cæsar's friendship, and served under him in Gaul, now joined Pompey. On the other hand, Cæsar was reduced to such straits both by sea and land that he was under the necessity of seeking a battle. Accordingly, he attacked Pompey's intrenchments and bade him defiance daily. In most of these attacks and skirmishes he had the advantage, but one day he was in danger of losing his whole army. Pompey fought with so much valor that he put Cæsar's whole detachment to flight, after having killed two thousand of them upon the spot, but was either unable or afraid to pursue his blow and enter their camp with them. Cæsar said to his friends on the occasion, "This day the victory had been the enemy's had their general known how to conquer."

Pompey's troops, elated with this success, were in great haste to come to a decisive battle. Nay, Pompey himself seemed to give in to their opinions by writing to the kings, the generals, and cities in his interest in the style of a conqueror. Yet all this while he dreaded the issue of a general action, believing it much better by length of time, by famine and fatigue, to tire out men who had been ever invincible in arms, and long accustomed to conquer when they fought together. Besides, he knew the infirmities of age had made them unfit for the other operations of war,—for long marches and countermarches, for digging trenches and building forts, and that, therefore, they wished for nothing so much as a battle. Pompey, with all these arguments, found it no easy matter to keep his army quiet.

Cæsar was preparing to march to Scotusa when his scouts brought intelligence that they had seen arms handed about in the enemy's camp, and perceived a noise and bustle, which indicated an approaching battle. After these others came and assured him that the first ranks were drawn up. Upon this Cæsar said, "The long-wished day is come on which we shall fight with men, and not with want and famine." Then he immediately ordered the red mantle to be put up before his pavilion, which, among the Romans, is the signal of a battle. The soldiers no sooner beheld it than they left their tents as they were, and ran to arms with loud shouts and every expression of joy; and when the officers began to put them in order of battle, each man fell into his proper rank as quietly and with as much skill and ease as a chorus in a tragedy.

Some of the principal Romans and Greeks who only stood and looked on when the dreadful moment of action approached, could not help considering to what the avarice and ambition of two men had brought the Roman Empire. The same arms on both sides, the troops marshaled in the same manner, the same standards; in short, the strength and flower of one and the same city turned upon itself! What could be a stronger proof of the blindness and infatuation of human nature when carried away by its passions? Had they been willing to enjoy the fruits of their labors in peace and tranquillity, the greatest and best part of the world was their own. Or, if they must have indulged their thirst of victories and triumphs, the Parthians and Germans were yet to be subdued, Scythia and India yet remained; together with a very plausible color for the lust of new acquisitions, the pretence of civilizing the barbarians. And what Scythian horse, what Parthian arrows, what Indian treasures, could have resisted seventy thousand Romans led on by Pompey and Cæsar, with whose names those nations had long been acquainted?

The plain of Pharsalia was now covered with men and horses and arms, and the signal of battle being given on both sides, the first on Cæsar's side who advanced to the charge was Caius Crastinus, who commanded a corps of a hundred and twenty men, and was determined to make good his promise to his general. He was the first man Cæsar saw when he went out of the trenches in the morning, and upon Cæsar's asking him what he thought of the battle, he stretched out his hand and answered in a cheerful tone, "You will gain a glorious victory, and I shall have your praise this day either alive or dead." In pursuance of this promise he advanced the foremost, and many following to support him, he charged into the midst of the enemy. They soon took to their swords, and numbers were slain; but as Crastinus was making his way forward, and cutting down all before him, one of Pompey's men stood to receive him, and pushed his sword in at his mouth with such force that it went through the nape of his neck. Crastinus thus killed, the fight was maintained with equal advantage on both sides.

Pompey did not immediately bring on his right wing, but often directed his eyes to the left, and lost time in waiting to see what execution his cavalry would do there. Meanwhile, they had extended their squadrons to surround Cæsar, and prepared to drive the few horse he had placed in front back upon the foot. At that instant Cæsar gave the signal, upon which his cavalry retreated a little, and six cohorts, which consisted of three thousand men, and had been placed behind the tenth legion, advanced to surround Pompey's cavalry, and coming close up to them raised the points of their javelins as they had been taught, and aimed them at the face. Their adversaries, who were not experienced in any kind of fighting, and had not the least previous idea of this, could not parry or endure the blows upon their faces, but turned their backs or covered their eyes with their hands, and soon fled with great dishonor. Cæsar's men took no care to pursue them, but turned their force upon the enemy's infantry, particularly upon that wing which, now stripped of its horse, lay open to the attack on all sides. The six cohorts, therefore, took them in flank, while the tenth legion charged them in front; and they who had hoped to surround the enemy, and now instead of that saw themselves surrounded, made but a short resistance, and then took to a precipitate flight.

By the great dust that was raised, Pompey saw the fate of his cavalry, and it is hard to say what passed in his mind at that moment. He appeared like a man moon-struck and distracted. When he had got at a little distance from the camp he quitted his horse. He had very few people about him, and as he saw he was not pursued he went softly on, wrapt up in such thoughts as we may suppose a man to have who had been used for thirty-four years to conquer and carry all before him, and now in his old age first came to know what it was to be defeated and to fly. We may easily conjecture what his thoughts must have been, when in one short hour he had lost the glory and the power which had been growing up amidst so many wars and conflicts; and he who was lately guarded with such armies of horse and foot, and such great and powerful fleets, was reduced to so mean and contemptible an equipage that his enemies who were in search of him could not know him.

Pompey took refuge in Egypt, but Ptolemy and his council were perplexed to know what to do with him. They were divided in their opinions, some advising the prince to give him an honorable reception, and others to send him an order to depart. But Theodotus, to display his eloquence, insisted that both were wrong. "If you receive him," said he, "you will have Cæsar for your enemy, and Pompey for your master. If you order him off, Pompey may one day revenge the affront, and Cæsar resent your not having put him in his hands. The best method, therefore, is to put him to death. By this means you will do Cæsar a favor, and have nothing to fear from Pompey." He added, with a smile, "Dead men do not bite."

This advice was followed, and Pompey was assassinated as he was landing from his galley. He was just 59 years old.

ALEXANDER.

Note.—ALEXANDER (Macedonian). Alexander was born B.C. 356. His life forms an epoch in the history of the world, and no biography can be more enthralling and instructive than that which follows. His death, in his thirty-third year, was due to inordinate excess in wine-drinking.

THIS famous general was descended from Hercules. His father was Philip, King of Macedonia, and his mother's name was Olympias.

The statues of Alexander that most resemble him were those of Lysippus, who alone had his permission to represent him in marble. The turn of his head, which leaned a little to one side, and the quickness of his eye, in which many of his friends and successors most affected to imitate him, were best hit off by that artist. Apelles painted him in the character of Jupiter armed with thunder, but did not succeed as to his complexion. He overcharged the coloring, and made his skin too brown; whereas he was fair, with a tinge of red in his face and upon his breast. We read that a most agreeable scent proceeded from his skin, and that his breath and whole body were fragrant. There was something superlatively great and sublime in his ambition far above his years. It was not all sorts of honor that he courted, nor did he seek it in every track like his father Philip, who was as proud of his eloquence as any sophist could be, and who had the vanity to record his victories in the Olympic chariot race in the impression of his coins. Alexander, on the other hand, when he was asked by some of the people about him, "Whether he would not run in the Olympic race?" (for he was swift of foot), answered, "Yes, if I had kings for my antagonists." It appears that he had a perfect aversion to the whole exercise of wrestling; for though he exhibited many other sorts of games and public diversions in which he proposed prizes for tragic poets, for musicians who practised upon the flute and lyre, and for rhapsodists too,—though he entertained the people with the hunting of all manner of wild beasts, and with fencing or fighting with the staff,—yet he gave no encouragement to boxing or to wrestling.

When a young horse, named Bucephalus, was offered for sale to Philip at the price of thirteen talents, the king, with the prince, and many others, went into the field to see some trial made of him. The horse appeared extremely vicious and unmanageable, and Philip was displeased at their bringing him so wild and ungovernable a horse, and bade them take him away. But Alexander, who had observed him well, said, "What a horse are they losing for want of skill and spirit to manage him!" Philip at first took no notice of this, but upon the prince's often repeating the same expression, and showing great uneasiness, he said, "Young man, you find fault with your elders as if you knew more than they, or could manage the horse better." "And I certainly could," answered the prince. "If you should not be able to ride him, what forfeiture will you submit to for your rashness?" "I will pay the price of the horse," said Alexander.

Upon this all the company laughed, but the king and prince agreeing as to the forfeiture, Alexander ran to the horse, and, laying hold on the bridle, turned him to the sun, for he had observed, it seems, that the shadow, which fell before the horse, and continually moved as he moved, greatly disturbed him. While his fierceness and fury lasted he kept speaking to him softly and stroking him; after which he gently let fall his mantle, leaped lightly upon his back, and got a safe seat. Then, without pulling the reins too hard, or using either whip or spur, he set him going. As soon as he perceived his uneasiness abated, and that he wanted only to run, he put him to a full gallop, and pushed him on both with the voice and the spur. Philip and all his court were in great distress for him at first, and a profound silence ensued. But when the prince had turned him, and brought him straight back, they all received him with loud acclamations except his father, who wept for joy, and kissing him, said, "Seek another kingdom, my son, that may be worthy of thy abilities, for Macedonia is too small for thee."

Alexander loved polite learning, and his thirst for knowledge made him a man of extensive reading. He called the *Iliad* of Homer a portable treasury of military knowledge, and he had a copy of the work corrected by Aristotle, which he used to lay beside his sword under his pillow. When Philip went on the expedition to Byzantium, Alexander was but sixteen years of age, but he was left Regent of Macedonia and Keeper of the Seal.

Philip was assassinated when Alexander was twenty years old. On succeeding to the crown he found the kingdom torn in pieces by dangerous parties. Having intelligence that the Thebans and Athenians had revolted, he resolved to show them that he was no longer a boy, and he immediately advanced through the Pass of Thermopylæ. Said he, "Demosthenes called me a boy while I was in Illyrium, and a stripling when in Thessaly, but I will show him before the walls of Athens that I am a man." Thebes was taken, and the city plundered and leveled with the ground.

A general assembly of the Greeks being held at the Isthmus of Corinth, they came to a resolution to send their quotas with Alexander against Darius, king of the Persians, and he was unanimously elected captain-general. Finding that Diogenes made but little account of Alexander, and that he preferred the enjoyment of his leisure in a part of the suburbs called Cranium, he went to see him. Diogenes happened to be lying in the sun, and, at the approach of so many people, he raised himself up a little and fixed his eyes upon Alexander. The king addressed him in an obliging manner, and asked him "if there was anything he could serve him in?" "Only stand a little out of my sunshine," said Diogenes. Alexander, we are told, was struck with such surprise at finding himself so little regarded, and saw something so great in that carelessness, that, while his courtiers were ridiculing the philosopher as a monster, he said, "If I were not Alexander I should wish to be Diogenes."

In the meantime Darius' generals had collected a great army on the banks of the Granicus. Many of Alexander's officers were afraid that the river was too deep to ford, but Alexander led the way, and managed to struggle across, and fought his way up the opposite bank. His army followed and defeated the barbarians. They lost in this battle twenty thousand foot and two thousand five hundred horse; whereas Alexander had no more than thirty-four men killed, nine of whom were infantry. To do honor to their memory he erected a statue to each of them in brass, the workmanship of Lysippus. And that the Greeks might have their share in the glory of the day, he sent them presents out of the spoil. To the Athenians in particular he sent three hundred bucklers. Upon the rest of the spoils he put this pompous inscription: "*Won by Alexander, the son of Philip, and the Greeks (excepting the Lacedæmonians) of the barbarians in Asia.*" The greatest part of the plate, the purple furniture, and other things of that kind which he took from the Persians, he sent to his mother.

His next acquisitions were Paphlagonia and Cappadocia. By this time Darius had taken his departure from Susa, full of confidence in his numbers; for his army consisted of six hundred thousand men. Alexander's progress was stayed by sickness. His physicians durst not give him any medicines, because they thought themselves not so certain of the cure as of the danger they must incur in the application. Philip, the Acarnanian, attempted the cure, and found no difficulty in persuading the king to wait with patience till his medicine was prepared.

In the mean time, Parmenio sent him a letter from the camp, advising him "to beware of Philip, whom," he said, "Darius had prevailed upon, by presents of infinite value, and the promise of his daughter in marriage, to take him off by poison." As soon as Alexander had read the letter he put it under his pillow, without showing it to any of his friends. The time appointed being come, Philip, with the king's friends, entered the chamber, having the cup which contained the medicine in his hand. The king received it freely without the least marks of suspicion, and at the same time put the letter in Philip's hands. It was a striking situation, and more interesting than any scene in a tragedy,—the one reading while the other was drinking. They looked upon each other, but with a very different air. The king, with an open and unembarrassed countenance, expressed his regard for Philip, and the confidence he had in his honor; Philip's look showed his indignation at the calumny.

The medicine, indeed, was so strong, and overpowered his spirits in such a manner, that at first he was speechless, but he was soon relieved, and his faithful physician had the gratification of seeing his patient well enough to march against Darius, and also to conquer him. The victory was a very signal one, for Alexander killed one hundred and ten thousand of the enemy, and nothing was wanted to complete it but the capture of Darius. That prince, however, escaped, leaving his wife and family captives. They were kindly and honorably treated by the conqueror.

After this Alexander had some rest, and enjoyed his leisure. He was not so much addicted to wine as he was thought to be. It was supposed so because he passed a great deal of time at table, but that time was spent rather in talking than drinking, every fresh cup introducing some long discourse. Besides, he never made these long meals but when he had abundance of leisure upon his hands. When business called he was not to be detained by wine, nor sleep, nor pleasure, nor honorable love, nor the most entertaining spectacle. On his leisure days, as soon as he was risen he sacrificed to the gods, after which he took his dinner sitting. The rest of the day he spent in hunting, or deciding the differences among his troops, or in reading and writing. If he was upon a march which did not require haste he would exercise himself in shooting and darting the javelin, or in mounting and alighting from a chariot at full speed. Sometimes also he diverted himself with fowling and fox-hunting. On his return to his quarters, when he went to be refreshed with the bath and with oil, he inquired of the stewards of his kitchen whether they had prepared everything in a handsome manner for supper. It was not till late in the evening, and when night was come on, that he took his meal, and then he ate in a recumbent posture. He was very attentive to his guests at table, that they might be served equally, and none neglected.

The siege of Tyre next occupied his attention; and having taken it, he marched to Syria, and laid siege to Gaza, the capital of that country, and took the city. He sent most of its spoils to Olympias and Cleopatra, and others of his friends. His tutor, Leonidas, was not forgotten; and the present he made him had something particular in it. It consisted of five hundred talents weight of frankincense, and a hundred talents of myrrh, and was sent upon the recollection of the hopes he had conceived when a boy. It seems Leonidas one day had observed Alexander, at a sacrifice, throwing incense into the fire by handfuls; upon which he said, "Alexander, when you have conquered the country where spices grow, you may be thus liberal of your incense; but, in the mean time, use what you have more sparingly." He, therefore, wrote thus:—" I have sent you frankincense and myrrh in abundance, that you may be no longer a churl to the gods."

A casket being one day brought him, which appeared to be one of the most curious and valuable among the treasures of Darius, he asked his friends what they thought most worthy to be put in it. Different things were proposed; but he said,

"The Iliad most deserved such a casket." And if what the Alexandrians say be true, Homer was no bad auxiliary or useless counselor in the course of the war. They tell us that when Alexander had conquered Egypt, and had determined to build there a great city, which was to be peopled with Greeks, and called Alexandria, after his own name, he traveled to Pharos, which at that time was an island lying a little above the Canobic mouth of the Nile, but now is joined to the mainland by a causeway. He no sooner cast his eyes upon the place than he perceived the commodiousness of the situation. On one side it has a great lake, and on the other the sea, which there forms a capacious harbor. He ordered a city to be planned on the ground; but for want of chalk the architects made use of flour of wheat, which answered well enough upon a black soil, but while the king was enjoying the design, a large number of birds of all kinds settled down on the lines, and ate up all the flour. Alexander was disturbed at the omen, but his diviners encouraged him to go on with the work by assuring him that it was a sign that the city he was going to build would be blessed with such plenty as to furnish a supply to all the nations which should repair to it. After marching across the desert, he returned to Macedonia. There he received a letter from Darius, in which that prince proposed, on condition of a pacification and future friendship, to pay him ten thousand talents in ransom of the prisoners; to cede to him all the countries on this side the

Euphrates; and to give him his daughter in marriage. Upon his communicating these proposals to his friends, Parmenio said, "If I were Alexander, I should accept them." "So would I," said Alexander, "if I were Parmenio." The answer he gave to Darius was, "If you will come to me, you shall find the best of treatment; if not, I must go and seek you." He therefore set off to seek for Darius, and, coming up with him, both sides prepared for the fight.

The great battle between Alexander and Darius was not fought at Arbela, as most historians will have it, but at Gangamela, which, in the Persian tongue, is said to signify *the house of the camel;* so called because one of the ancient kings, having escaped his enemies by the swiftness of his camel, placed her there, and appointed the revenue of certain villages for her maintenance.

In the month of September there happened an eclipse of the moon, about the beginning of the festival of the great mysteries at Athens. The eleventh night after that eclipse, the two armies being in view of each other, Darius kept his men under arms, and took a general review of his troops by torchlight. Meantime Alexander suffered his Macedonians to repose themselves, and with his soothsayer Aristander performed some private ceremonies before his tent, and offered sacrifices to Fear. The oldest of his friends, and Parmenio in particular, when they beheld the plain between Niphates and the Gordæan Mountains all illuminated with the torches of the barbarians, and heard the tumultuous and appalling noise from their camp like the roarings of an immense sea, were astonished at their numbers, and observed among themselves how arduous an enterprise it would be to meet such a torrent of war in open day. They waited upon the king, therefore, when he had finished the sacrifice, and advised him to attack the enemy in the night, when darkness would hide what was most dreadful in the combat. Upon which he gave them that celebrated answer, "I will not steal a victory."

When the morning came, after sacrificing, Alexander put on his helmet, being otherwise ready armed. He wore a short coat of the Sicilian fashion girt close about him, and over that a breastplate of linen strongly quilted, which was found among the spoils at the battle of Issus. His helmet was of iron, but so well polished that it shone like the brightest silver. To this was fitted a gorget of the same metal, set with precious stones. His sword, the weapon he generally used in battle, was a present from the king of the Citieans, and could not be excelled for lightness or for temper. But the belt which he wore in all engagements was more superb than the rest of his armor. It was given him by the Rhodians as a mark of their respect, and old Helicon had exerted all his art on it. In drawing up his army and giving orders, as well as exercising and reviewing it, he spared Bucephalus on account of his age, and rode another horse; but he constantly charged on him, and Alexander had no sooner mounted him than the signal for battle was always given. In the battle Darius was beaten, and had to fly; and his grand army was totally routed. Alexander was acknowledged king of all Asia.

Having nothing to occupy them, Alexander found that his great officers set no bounds to their luxury; that they were most extravagantly delicate in their diet, and profuse in other respects; insomuch that Agnon of Teos wore silver nails in his shoes; Leonatus had many camel-loads of earth brought from Egypt to rub himself with when he went to the wrestling ring; Philotas had hunting nets that would inclose the space of a hundred furlongs; more made use of rich essences than oil after bathing, and had their grooms of the bath, as well as chamberlains who excelled in bed-making. This degeneracy he reproved with all the temper of a philosopher. He told them it was very strange to him that, after having undergone so many glorious conflicts, they did not remember that those who come from labor and exercise always sleep more sweetly than the inactive and effeminate; and that in comparing the Persian manners with the Macedonian they did not perceive that nothing was more servile than the love of pleasure, or more princely than a life of toil. "How will that man," continued he, "take care of his own horse, or furbish his lance and helmet, whose hands are too delicate to wait on his own dear person? Know you not that the end of conquest is, not to do what the conquered have done, but something greatly superior?"

When Alexander marched against Darius again, he expected another battle; but the Persian monarch fled. The pursuit was long and laborious; for he rode 3,300 furlongs in eleven days.* They were all eager to keep up with Alexander, but only sixty men were able to keep up with him till he reached the enemy's camp. There they rode over the gold and silver that lay scattered about, and passing by a number of carriages which were in motion, full of women and children, but without charioteers, they hastened to the leading squadrons, not doubting that they should find Darius among them. At last, after much search, they found him extended on his chariot and pierced with many darts. Though he was near his last moments he had strength to ask for something to quench his thirst. A Macedonian, named Polystratus, brought him some cold water, and when he had drank, he said, "Friend, this fills up the measure of my misfortunes, to think I am not able to reward thee for this act of kindness. But Alexander will not let thee go without a recompense; and the gods will reward him for his humanity to my mother, to my wife, and children. Tell him I gave him my hand, for I give it thee in his stead." So saying, he took the hand of Polystratus, and immediately expired. When Alexander came up he showed his concern for that event by the strongest expressions, and covered the body with his own robe. As for the body of Darius, he ordered it should have all the honors of a royal funeral, and sent it embalmed to his mother.

* Three hundred miles.

As to the war with the Indian prince Porus, it was carried on with the usual extraordinary energy. Most historians agree that Porus was four cubits and a span high; and that, though the elephant he rode was one of the largest, his stature and bulk were such that he appeared but proportionably mounted. This elephant, during the whole battle, gave extraordinary proofs of his sagacity and care of the king's person. As long as that prince was able to fight he defended him with great courage, and repulsed all assailants; and when he perceived him ready to sink under the multitude of darts and the wounds with which he was covered, to prevent his falling off he kneeled down in the softest manner and with his proboscis gently drew every dart out of his body.

In the battle with Porus, Alexander's favorite horse, Bucephalus received several wounds, of which he afterward died, being thirty years old. Alexander showed as much regret as if he had lost a faithful friend and companion—he esteemed him, indeed, as such—and built a city near the Hydaspes, in the place where he was buried, which he called after him, Bucephalia. He is also reported to have built a city and called it Peritas, in memory of a dog of that name which he had brought up and was very fond of.

The Macedonians refused to follow Alexander to the banks of the Ganges, which grieved him greatly, and he was very indignant, considering that a retreat was nothing less than an acknowledgment that he was overcome. On his return march he attacked many cities, and was always victorious. He was, however, very near being cut in pieces by the Malli, who were called the most warlike people in India. He had driven some of them from the walls of their city with his missive weapons, and was the first man that ascended it. But presently, after he was up, the scaling-ladder broke. Finding himself and his small company much galled by the darts of the barbarians from below, he poised himself and leaped down into the midst of the enemy. By good fortune he fell upon his feet, and the barbarians were so astonished at the flashing of his arms as he came down that they thought they beheld lightning or some supernatural splendor issuing from his body. At first, therefore, they drew back and dispersed; but when they had collected themselves, and saw him attended only by two of his guards, they attacked him hand to hand, and wounded him through his armor with their swords and spears, notwithstanding the valor with which he fought. One of them standing farther off, drew an arrow with such strength that it made its way through his cuirass, and entered the ribs under the breast. Its force was so great that he was brought upon his knees, and the barbarian ran up with his drawn scimiter to dispatch him, when Peucestes and Limnæus placed themselves before him; but the one was wounded and the other killed. Peucestes, who survived, was still making some resistance, when Alexander recovered himself and laid the barbarian at his feet. The king, however, received new wounds; and at last had such a blow from a bludgeon upon his neck that he was forced to support himself by the wall, and there stood with his face to the enemy. The Macedonians, who by this time had got in, gathered about him, and carried him off to his tent. He had lost his senses, and it was the current report in the army that he was dead. When they had with great difficulty sawn off the shaft of the arrow, and with equal trouble had taken off the cuirass, they proceeded to extract the arrow head, which stuck fast in the bone. Alexander fainted under the operation, and was very near expiring; but when the head was got out he recovered.

His next expedition was to Persia, and the first thing he did on entering that kingdom was to give money to the matrons, according to the ancient custom of the kings, who, upon their return to their Persian dominions from any excursion, used to give every woman a piece of gold. Having found the tomb of Cyrus broken open, he put the author of that sacrilege to death, though a native of Pella, and a person of some distinction. His name was Polymachus. After he had read the epitaph, which was in the Persian language, he ordered it to be inscribed also in Greek. It was as follows:—*O man! whosoever thou art, and whencesoever thou comest, for come I know thou wilt, I am Cyrus, the founder of the Persian Empire. Envy me not the little earth that covers my body.* Alexander was much affected at these words, which placed before him in so strong a light the vicissitudes of fortune.

When he came to Ecbatana in Media, and had dispatched the most urgent affairs, he employed himself again in the celebration of games and other public solemnities; for which purpose three thousand artificers, lately arrived from Greece, were very serviceable to him. But unfortunately Hephæstion fell sick of a fever in the midst of this festivity. As a young man and a soldier he could not bear to be kept to strict diet, and taking the opportunity to dine when his physician Glaucus was gone to the theater, he ate a roasted fowl, and drank a flagon of wine made as cold as possible; in consequence of which he grew worse and died a few days after. Alexander's grief on this occasion exceeded all bounds. He immediately ordered the horses and mules to be shorn, that they might have their share in the mourning, and with the same view pulled down the battlements of the neighboring cities, and he crucified the poor physician.

When once Alexander had given himself up to superstition his mind was so preyed upon by vain fears and anxieties that he turned the least incident which was anything strange and out of the way into a sign or a portent. The Court swarmed with sacrificers, purifiers, and prognosticators; they were all to be seen exercising their talents there. So true it is, that though the disbelief of religion and contempt of things divine is a great evil, yet superstition is a greater; for as water gains upon low grounds, so superstition prevails over a dejected mind, and fills it with fear and folly. This was entirely Alexander's case. However, upon the receipt of some oracles concerning Hephæstion from the god he commonly consulted, he gave a truce to his sorrows, and employed himself in festive sacrifices and entertainments.

One day, after he had given Nearchus a sumptuous treat, he went, according to custom, to refresh himself in the bath in order to retire to rest. But, in the meantime, Medius came and invited him to take part in a carousal, and he could not deny him. There he drank all that night and the next day, till at last he found a fever coming upon him. He then took a draft of wine which threw him into a frenzy, and he died on the 30th June, B.C. 323.

JULIUS CÆSAR.

Note.—JULIUS CÆSAR (Roman). This man, one of the greatest in all history, was born B.C. 100, and was descended from the Julian family. When only sixteen years old, he lost his father who was Prætor. Some time later, Cæsar married Cornelia, daughter of Lucius Cinna. This so offended Sylla that he secured the proscription of Cæsar, unwillingly releasing him some time later from the effects of the decree. The career of Cæsar is fully told by Plutarch.

THE earliest incident in the life of Julius Cæsar was his capture by pirates. They demanded a ransom of only twenty talents, which he soon obtained, but immediately manned some vessels and attacked the corsairs. He captured and crucified the whole of them.

When the power of Sylla began to decline, Cæsar's friends pressed him to return to Rome. But he first went to Rhodes to study under Apollonius, the son of Molon, who taught rhetoric there. Cicero also was one of his scholars. Cæsar is said to have had happy talents from nature for a public speaker, and he did not lack the ambition to cultivate them; so that undoubtedly he was the second orator in Rome, and he might have been the first had he not rather chosen pre-eminence in arms. Hence it was that afterward, in his Anti-Cato, which he wrote in answer to a book of Cicero's, he desired his readers—"Not to expect, in the performance of a military man, the style of a complete orator who had bestowed all his time upon such studies."

When Cæsar had been elected Prætor, the government of Spain was allotted to him. But his circumstances were so indifferent, and his creditors so clamorous and troublesome, that when he was preparing for his departure he was forced to apply to Crassus, the richest man in Rome, who stood in need of Cæsar's warmth and vigor to keep up the balance of power against Pompey. Crassus, therefore, took upon him to pay the most inexorable of his creditors, and became responsible for eight hundred and thirty talents, which procured for Cæsar liberty to set out for his province.

On his return to Rome he went to work upon an expedient which deceived all the world except

Cato. It was the reconciliation of Pompey and Crassus, two of the most powerful men in Rome. By making them friends Cæsar secured to himself the interest of both. And while he seemed to be only doing an office of humanity he was undermining the constitution. Cæsar and Pompey first combined to ruin the authority of the senate; and when that was effected, they parted to pursue each his own designs. Cato, who often prophesied what would be the consequence, was then looked upon as a troublesome and over-busy man; but afterward he was esteemed a wise though not a fortunate counselor.

As a warrior Cæsar was not in the least inferior to the greatest and most admired commanders the world ever produced; for whether we compare him with the Fabii, the Scipios, and Metelli, with the generals of his own time, or with those who flourished a little before him, as Sylla, Marius, the two Luculli, or with Pompey himself, whose fame in every military excellence reached the skies, Cæsar's achievements bear away the palm. One he surpassed in the difficulty of the scene of action; another, in the extent of the countries he subdued; this, in the number and strength of the enemies he overcame; that, in the savage manners and treacherous disposition of the people he humanized. One he excelled in mildness and clemency to his prisoners; another, in bounty and munificence to his troops; and all, in the number of battles that he won and the enemies he killed. For in the war in Gaul, in less than ten years, he took eight hundred cities by assault, conquered three hundred states, and fought pitched battles, at different times, with three millions of men; one million of which he destroyed, and made another million prisoners. Such, moreover, was the affection of his soldiers, and their attachment to his person, that they, who under other commanders were nothing above the common rate of men, became invincible where Cæsar's glory was concerned, and they met the most dreadful dangers with a courage that nothing could resist. He seemed to know no fear, and his patience was astounding, especially as he was of a delicate constitution and subject to violent headaches and epileptic fits. He did not, however, make these disorders a pretence for indulging himself. On the contrary, he sought in war a remedy for his infirmities, endeavoring to strengthen his constitution by long marches, by simple diet, and by seldom going under cover. Upon a march, when he slept it was commonly either in a chariot or a litter, that rest might be no hindrance to business. In the day-time he visited the castles, cities, and fortified camps, with his servant at his side, whom he employed, on such occasions, to write for him, and with a soldier behind who carried his sword. By these means he traveled so fast, and with so little interruption, as to reach the Rhone in eight days after his first setting out for those parts from Rome. He was a good horseman from his early years, and brought that exercise to such perfection by practice that he could sit a horse at full speed with his hands behind him. In this expedition he also accustomed himself to dictate letters as he rode on horseback, and found sufficient employment for two secretaries at once, or, according to Oppius, for more. It is also said that Cæsar was the first who contrived to communicate his thoughts by letter to his friends who were in the same city with him, when any urgent affair required it, and the multiplicity of business or great extent of the city did not admit of an interview.

Of his indifference with respect to diet we have this remarkable proof:—Happening to sup with Valerius Leo, a friend of his, at Milan, there was sweet ointment poured upon the asparagus instead of oil. Cæsar ate of it freely notwithstanding, and afterward rebuked his friends for expressing their dislike of it. "It was enough," said he, "to forbear eating if it was disagreeable to you. He who finds fault with any rusticity is himself a rustic." Cæsar was very anxious to be the first man who should cross the Rhine in a hostile manner, and, in spite of the Germans who inhabited the banks of the river, he took his army over and laid the country waste.

But his expedition into Britain discovered the most daring spirit of enterprise, for he was the first who entered the Western ocean with a fleet, and having embarked his troops on the Atlantic, he carried war into an island whose very existence was doubted. Some writers had represented it as incredibly large, and others contested its being. Yet Cæsar attempted to conquer it, and to extend the Roman Empire beyond the bounds of the known world. He sailed twice from the opposite coast in Gaul to Britain, and fought many battles, by which the Britons suffered more than the Romans gained; for there was nothing worth taking from a people who were so poor and lived in so much wretchedness. He did not, however, terminate the war in the manner he could have wished; he only received hostages of the King of Britain, and appointed the tribute the island was to pay, and then returned to Rome.

Cæsar had long resolved to ruin Pompey, and Pompey to destroy Cæsar. For Crassus, who alone could have taken up the conqueror, being killed in the Parthian war, there remained nothing for Cæsar to do, to make himself the greatest of mankind, but to annihilate him who was so; nor for Pompey to prevent it, but to take off the man he feared. By long service and great achievements in the wars of Gaul he had so improved his army, and his own reputation too, that he was considered as on a footing with Pompey; and he found pretenses for carrying his enterprise into execution in the times of the misgovernment at Rome. These were partly furnished by Pompey himself; and, indeed, all ranks of men were so corrupted that tables were publicly set out upon which the candidates for offices were professedly ready to pay the people the price of their votes; and the people came not only to give their voices for the man who had bought them, but with all manner of offensive weapons to fight for him.

Hence it often happened that they did not part without polluting the tribunal with blood and murder, and the city was a perpetual scene of anarchy.

When Cæsar and Pompey had each raised a large army, and several fruitless attempts had been made to reconcile them, Cæsar at last proposed to lay down his arms on condition that Pompey should do the same. The question was put to the senate, but they could come to no conclusion, and on account of this unhappy discussion all ranks of people put on black as in a time of public mourning. Civil war soon broke out in Rome, and Cæsar determined to march his army toward the city. When he arrived at the banks of the Rubicon, the river which divides Cisalpine Gaul from the rest of Italy, his reflections became more interesting in proportion as the danger drew near. Staggered by the greatness of his attempt, he stopped to weigh with himself its inconveniences, and, as he stood considering the arguments on both sides, he many times changed his opinion. After which he deliberated upon it with such of his friends as were by, enumerating the calamities which the passage of that river would bring upon the world, and the reflections that might be made by posterity upon it. At last, upon some sudden impulse, bidding adieu to his reasonings, and plunging into the abyss of futurity, in the words of those who embark in doubtful and arduous enterprises, he cried out, "The die is cast!" and immediately passed the Rubicon.

Pompey fled, closely pursued by Cæsar, and in the short space of sixty days the latter found himself master of the whole of Italy without having spilled one drop of blood. Then finding Rome in a more settled condition than he expected, and many senators there, he addressed them in a mild and gracious manner, and desired them to send deputies to Pompey to offer honorable terms of peace. But not one of them would take upon him the commission. As Metellus, the tribune, opposed his taking money out of the public treasury, and alleged some laws against it, Cæsar said, "Arms and laws do not flourish together. If you are not pleased at what I am about, you have nothing to do but to withdraw; indeed, war will not bear much liberty of speech. When I say this, I am departing from my own right; for you, and all whom I have found exciting a spirit of faction against me, are at my disposal." Saying this, he approached the doors of the treasury, and as the keys were not produced he sent for workmen to break the doors open. Cæsar then resumed his march against Pompey, and after a desperate battle at Pharsalia completely routed him.

When Cæsar reached Alexandria he found that Pompey had been assassinated. During his stay in Egypt he was forced to burn his ships to prevent their falling into the hands of the enemy, and the flames unfortunately spread from the dock to the palace, and the great Alexandrian library was burned. Subsequently, in a sea fight near the isle of Pharos, seeing his men hard-pressed, he leaped into a little skiff to go to their assistance. The Egyptians making up on all sides, he threw himself into the sea, and with much difficulty reached his galleys by swimming. Having several valuable papers, which he was not willing either to lose or to wet, it is said he held them above water with one hand, and swam with the other. At last Cæsar attacked and defeated the king. Great numbers of the Egyptians were slain, and the king was heard of no more. This gave Cæsar an opportunity of establishing Cleopatra as Queen of Egypt.

He then departed for Syria, and from thence marched into Asia Minor. Cæsar immediately marched against Pharnaces with three legions, and defeated him in a great battle near Zela, which deprived him of the kingdom of Pontus, as well as ruined his whole army. In the account he gave Amintius, one of his friends in Rome, of the rapidity and dispatch with which he gained his victory, he made use only of three words, "*Veni, vidi, vici*" (I came, I saw, I conquered). Their having all the same form and termination in the Roman language adds grace to their conciseness.

Cæsar, after his return from Africa to Rome, spoke in high terms of his victory to the people. He told them he had subdued a country so extensive that it would bring yearly into the public stores two hundred thousand Attic measures of wheat, and three million of pounds of oil. After this he led up his several triumphs over Egypt, Pontus, and Africa.

Soon after he had been elected consul the fourth time, the first thing he undertook was to march into Spain against the sons of Pompey, who, though young, had assembled a numerous army, and showed a courage worthy the command they had undertaken. The great battle which put a period to that war was fought under the walls of Munda. Cæsar at first saw his men so hard-pressed, and making so feeble a resistance, that he ran through the ranks amidst the swords and spears, crying, "Are you not ashamed to deliver your general into the hands of boys?" The great and vigorous efforts this reproach produced at last made the enemy turn their backs, and there were more than thirty thousand of them slain; whereas Cæsar lost only a thousand, but those were some of the best men he had. As he retired after the battle he told his friends—"He had often fought for victory, but that was the first time he had fought for his life."

The younger of Pompey's sons made his escape; the other was taken a few days after by Didius, who brought his head to Cæsar.

This was the last of his wars; and his triumph on account of it gave the Romans more pain than any other step he had taken. He did not now mount the car for having conquered foreign generals or barbarian kings, but for ruining the children and destroying the race of one of the greatest men Rome had ever produced; and all the world condemned his triumphing in the calamities of his country.

Amongst many important things which Cæsar did, it should not be forgotten that he completed the regulation of the calendar, and corrected the erroneous computations of time.

The principal cause of the public hatred against him was his passion for the title of king. He also treated the tribunes with great indignity, till at last a conspiracy was formed to kill him. One day, when Cæsar entered the senate house, the senators rose up to do him honor as usual; but the conspirators surrounded him with drawn swords. Casca gave the first blow; many others followed; for it had been agreed that all should share in the deed. Therefore Brutus himself gave him a stroke in the groin. Some say he opposed the rest, and continued struggling and crying out till he perceived the sword of Brutus; then he drew his robe over his face and yielded to his fate. Either by accident, or pushed thither by the conspirators, he expired on the pedestal of Pompey's statue, and dyed it with his blood: so that Pompey seemed to preside over the work of vengeance, to tread his enemy under his feet, and to enjoy his agonies. Those agonies were great, for he received no less than three-and-twenty **wounds.** Cæsar died at the age of fifty-six, B.C. 44.

PHOCION.

Note.—PHOCION (Greek). Phocion was born about B.C. 400. What more striking proof of his success as a soldier need be asked than the fact that he was appointed general forty-five times? His private character was stainless, but his political course was infamous.

WHEN Phocion was very young he was in tuition with Plato, and afterward with Xenocrates in the academy; and from the very first he distinguished himself by his strong application to the most valuable studies. If he made an excursion into the country, or marched out to war, he went always barefooted, and without his upper garment too, except it happened to be intolerably cold; and then his soldiers used to laugh, and say, "It is a sign of a sharp winter; Phocion has got his clothes on." He was one of the most humane and best-tempered men in the world, and yet he had so ill-natured and forbidding a look that strangers were afraid to address him without company. Therefore, when Chares, the orator, observed to the Athenians what terrible brows Phocion had, and they could not help making themselves merry, he said, "This brow of mine never gave one of you an hour of sorrow; but the laughter of these sneerers has cost their country many a tear." In like manner, though the measures he proposed were happy ones, and his counsels of the most salutary kind, yet he used no flowers of rhetoric; his speeches were concise, commanding, and severe. For, as Zeno rightly says, a philosopher should never let a word come out of his mouth that is not strongly tinctured with sense; so Phocion's oratory contained the most sense in the fewest words. And it seems that Polyeuctus had this in view when he said, "Demosthenes was the better orator, and Phocion the more persuasive speaker." His speeches were to be estimated like coins, not for the size, but for the intrinsic value. The general amiability of his character obtained for him the surname of "The Good." He was a capable general; but his enemies conspired against him and accused him of treason. He was ordered to be poisoned with several other Athenians.

When they came to drink the poison, the quantity proved insufficient, and the executioner refused to prepare more unless he had twelve drachmas paid him. As this occasioned a troublesome delay, Phocion called one of his friends, and said, "Since one cannot die free of cost at Athens, give the man his money." This execution was on the 19th day of April, B.C. 318.

CATO, THE YOUNGER.

Note.—CATO, THE YOUNGER (Roman). Cato the Younger was born B.C. 95, and began his military career B.C. 72 as volunteer. He was elected quæstor B.C. 65. Before stabbing himself to death, as related below, he withdrew to his chamber and read Plato's dialogue on "the Immortality of the Soul."

WE are told that Cato from his infancy showed in his voice, his look, and his very diversions, a firmness and solidity which neither passion nor anything else could move. He pursued every object he had in view with a vigor far above his years, and a resolution that nothing could resist. Those who were inclined to flatter were sure to meet with a severe repulse; and to those who attempted to intimidate him he was still more intractable. Scarcely anything could make him laugh, and it was but rarely that his countenance was softened to a smile. He was not quickly or easily moved to anger; but it was difficult to appease his resentment when once excited.

His apprehension was slow, and his learning came with difficulty; but what he had once learned he long retained. The inflexibility of his disposition seems to have retarded his progress in learning. Yet Cato is said to have been very obedient to his preceptor, and to have done whatever he was commanded; only he would always inquire the reason, and ask why such and such a thing was enjoined. Indeed, Sarpedon, his preceptor, was a man of engaging manners, who chose rather to govern by reason than by violence. Cato was very fond of his brother Cæpio, and was never happy but when he was by his side.

To strengthen his constitution, he practiced the most laborious exercises. He accustomed himself to go bareheaded in the hottest and coldest weather, and traveled on foot at all seasons of the year. His friends who traveled with him made use of horses, and he joined sometimes one and sometimes another for conversation as he went along. In time of sickness his patience and abstinence were extraordinary. If he happened to have a fever he spent the whole day alone, suffering no person to approach him till he found a sensible change for the better. At entertainments they threw the dice for the choice of the messes; and if Cato lost the first choice, his friends used to offer it him, but he always refused it.

By the death of a cousin he came into a large estate; and when his friends wanted to borrow he lent them money without interest; and when the borrowers exhausted his ready money, he mortgaged his own slaves and his land to enable himself to continue lending.

Cato prided himself in being a Stoic, and took great delight in studying Plato's works. Toward the close of his life his mind seemed to give way, and he stabbed himself when he was about 50 years old, B.C. 46.

AGIS.

Note.—AGIS (Spartan). The name of Agis was borne by four kings of Sparta. The son of Eudamides was a lineal descendant of Agesilaus. His death occurred B.C. 241.

AGIS was a celebrated king of Sparta, the son of Eudamides. He excelled almost all the kings who reigned before him since the great Agesilaus in goodness of disposition and dignity of mind. For though brought up in the greatest affluence, and in all the indulgence that might be expected from female tuition under his mother Agesistrata and his grandmother Archidamia, who were the richest persons in Lacedæmonia, yet before he reached the age of twenty he declared war against pleasure. To prevent any vanity which the beauty of his person might have suggested he discarded all unnecessary ornament and expense, and constantly appeared in a plain Lacedæmonian cloak. In his diet, his bathing, and in all his exercises, he kept close to the Spartan simplicity; and he often used to say that he only wanted the crown that it might enable him to restore the laws and ancient discipline of his country.

When he ascended the throne he strove hard to improve the condition of the Spartans, and won the affections of his people; but his success only provoked the ephori to oppose his measures. One of them, Leonidas by name, raised a conspiracy against him, and one day he was arrested by arrangement near the prison. At the same time, Demochares, who was a tall, strong man, wrapped his cloak about the king's head, and dragged him off. The rest, as they had previously concerted the thing, pushed him on behind; and no one coming to his rescue or assistance, he was committed to prison.

Leonidas presently came with a strong band of mercenaries to secure the prison without; and the ephori entered it with such senators as were of their party. They began, as in a judicial process, with demanding what he had to say in defense of his proceedings; and as the young prince only laughed at their dissimulation, Amphares told him "they would soon make him weep for his presumption." Another of the ephori, seeming inclined to put him in a way of excusing himself and getting off, asked him, "Whether Lysander and Agesilaus had not forced him into the measures he took?" But Agis answered, "I was forced by no man; it was my attachment to the institutions of Lycurgus, and my desire to imitate him, which made me adopt his form of government." Then the same magistrate demanded, "Whether he repented of what he had done?" and his answer was, "I shall never repent of so glorious a design, though I see death before my eyes." Upon this they passed sentence of death upon him, and commanded the officers to carry him into the decade, which is a small apartment in the prison where they strangle malefactors. But the officers durst not touch him, and the mercenaries declined to do so; for they thought it impious to lay violent hands on a king. Demochares, seeing this, loaded them with reproaches, and threatened to punish them. At the same time he laid hold on Agis himself, and thrust him into the dungeon.

By this time it was generally known that Agis was taken into custody, and there was a great concourse of people at the prison gates with lanterns and torches. Among the numbers who resented these proceedings were the mother and grandmother of Agis, crying out and begging that the king might be heard and judged by the people in full assembly. But this, instead of procuring him a respite, hastened his execution; for they were afraid he would be rescued in the night if the tumult should increase.

As Agis was going to execution he perceived one of the officers lamenting his fate with tears; upon which he said, "My friend, dry up your tears; for as I suffer innocently I am in a better condition than those who condemn me contrary to law and justice." So saying, he cheerfully offered his neck to the executioner.

CLEOMENES.

Note.—CLEOMENES (Spartan). The defeat of Cleomenes at Sellasia took place B.C. 222. His suicide followed three years later. There were others who bore the name of Cleomenes, but they were of inferior note.

THE King Cleomenes about whom we are writing was the third of that name who had sat on the throne of Sparta. He was ambitious to gain glory, and had a native greatness of mind. He was not satisfied with the prevailing manners and customs of Sparta, for he observed that ease and pleasure were the great objects of the people. He noticed that individuals, entirely actuated by self-interest, paid no attention to the business of the state any further than they could turn it to their own emolument.

When Leonidas died, and Cleomenes came to the throne he observed that all ranks of men were utterly corrupted. The rich had an eye only to private profit and pleasure, and utterly neglected the public interest. The common people, on account of the meanness of their circumstances, had no spirit for war, or ambition to instruct their children in the Spartan exercises. Cleomenes himself had only the name of king, while the power was in the hands of the ephori. He therefore soon began to think of changing this state of affairs, and the readiest way seemed to be by getting rid of the ephori. He endeavored to convince his father-in-law, Megistonus, that the yoke of the ephori ought to be broken, and an equal division of property made; by means of which equality Sparta would resume her ancient valor and prestige. Megistonus complied, and the king then took two or three other friends into the scheme. Soon after, all the ephori but one were put to death. He was one of the first who gave up his own estate to the public stock, and his father-in-law and many friends followed his example. The whole of the citizens readily joined in the scheme, and the land was re-allotted. Then all the old Spartan laws and customs were again established, and the king himself was plain and simple in his equipage and diet, assuming no manner of pomp above a common citizen; he set a glorious example of sobriety.

His common supper was short and truly laconic. There were only couches for three people; but when he entertained ambassadors or strangers, two more couches were added, and the table was a little better furnished by the servants; not that any curious dessert was added, only the dishes were larger and the wine more generous; for he blamed one of his friends for setting nothing before strangers but the coarse cake and black broth which they ate in their common refectories. "When we have strangers to entertain," he said, "we need not be such very exact Lacedæmonians." After supper a three-legged stand was brought in, upon which were placed a brass bowl full of wine, two silver pots that held about a pint and a half apiece, and a few other cups. Such of the guests as were inclined to drink made use of these vessels; for the cup was not pressed upon any man against his will. There was no music or other amusement, nor was any such thing wanted. He entertained his company very agreeably with his own conversation—sometimes asking questions, and sometimes telling stories.

He raised a small army only at first, but he was soon obliged to increase it, and to march against enemies on all sides. He took Argos after a desperate struggle, and recovered the whole of Peloponnesus.

The tide of success then turned against Cleomenes, and he was in great straits for want of money. He was defeated and ruined at the battle of Sellasia by Antigonus. He sought refuge in Egypt, and was taken, by orders of Ptolemy Euergetes, to Alexandria, where he was treated with some degree of consideration; but old Ptolemy died before he could put his intentions in favor of Cleomenes into execution, and his successor on the Egyptian throne was no friend to Cleomenes. The ex-king of Sparta and his friends then took means to escape from Egypt; but they were caught before they could get to their ships, and in their extreme trouble all of them committed suicide. Cleomenes had been king of Sparta sixteen years.

Ptolemy was no sooner informed of what had happened than he ordered the body of Cleomenes to be flayed and nailed to a cross, and his children and mother and companions to be put to death. A few days after, the soldiers who watched the body of Cleomenes on the cross saw a great snake winding about his head and covering all his face, so that no bird of prey durst touch it. This struck Ptolemy with superstitious terror, and made way for the women to try a variety of expiations; for he was now persuaded that he had caused the death of a person who was a favorite of heaven, and something more than mortal. The Alexandrians crowded to the place, and called Cleomenes a hero, a son of the gods, till the philosophers put a stop to their devotions by assuring them that as dead oxen breed bees, horses wasps, and beetles rise out of the putrefaction of asses, so human carcasses (when some of the moisture of the marrow is evaporated, and it comes to a thicker consistence) produce serpents. The ancients, knowing this doctrine, appropriated the serpent, rather than any other animal, to heroes.

TIBERIUS GRACCHUS.

Note.—TIBERIUS GRACCHUS (Roman). This famous tribune and reformer was born about B.C. 166. As stated below, he was less than thirty years of age at his death.

HAVING given the history of Agis and Cleomenes, we have two Romans to compare with them, namely Tiberius and Caius Gracchus. They were the sons of Tiberius Gracchus.

Tiberius, as he grew toward manhood, gained so extraordinary a reputation that he was admitted into the college of the augurs, rather on account of his virtue than his high birth. He was soon after made a tribune, but when he sought re-election he was strongly opposed, and when the day of election came the person who had care of the chickens which were used in augury brought them out and set food before them, but none of them came out of the pen except one, and that one would not eat; it only raised its left wing, stretched out a leg, and then went in again. This put Tiberius in mind of a former ill omen. He had a helmet that he wore in battle, finely ornamented, and remarkably magnificent; two serpents that had crept into it privately laid their eggs and hatched in it. Such a bad presage made him more afraid of the late one. Yet he set out for the capitol, as soon as he understood that the people were assembled there. But in going out of his house he stumbled upon the threshold, and struck it with so much violence that the nail of his great toe was broken, and the blood flowed from the wound. When he had got a little on his way, he saw on his left hand two ravens fighting on the top of a house; and though he was attended, on account of his dignity, by great numbers of people, a stone which one of the ravens dropped fell close by his foot. This startled even the boldest of his partisans. But one of his train said, "It would be an unsupportable disgrace if Tiberius, the son of Gracchus, grandson of Scipio Africanus, and protector of the people of Rome, should, for fear of a raven, disappoint that people when they called him to their assistance."

Tiberius soon discovered that the people having landed interests had applied to the magistrates to protect them; but as they could not prevail, they had resolved to dispatch him, Tiberius, themselves, and for that purpose had armed themselves and their friends and slaves. Tiberius no sooner communicated this intelligence to those about him, than they tucked up their gowns, seized the halberts with which the sergeants kept off the crowd, broke them, and took the pieces to ward off any assault that might be made. Such as were at a distance, much surprised at seeing this, asked what the reason might be, and Tiberius, finding they could not hear him, touched his head with his hand to signify the danger he was in. His adversaries seeing this, ran and informed the senators that Tiberius demanded the diadem, alleging that gesture as a proof of it.

A riot ensued, and there was a serious fight. The attendants had brought clubs and bludgeons with them from home, and the patricians seized the feet of the benches which the populace had broken in their flight. Thus armed, they made toward Tiberius, knocking down such as stood before him. These being killed or dispersed, Tiberius likewise fled. He happened, however, to stumble and fall over some of the killed. As he was recovering himself, one of his colleagues came up openly, and struck him on the head with the foot of a stool, and another gave him a blow which killed him. More than three hundred persons lost their lives in this affray with clubs, stones, and like weapons; but not one was killed by the sword. This is said to have been the first instance of sedition in Rome, since the expulsion of the kings, which caused blood to be shed.

Tiberius Gracchus was only twenty-nine years old when he died.

CAIUS GRACCHUS.

Note.—CAIUS GRACCHUS (Roman). Caius Gracchus was a younger brother of Tiberius Gracchus and was born about B.C. 157. After his brother's death he lived in retirement until his death B.C. 126.

THIS Roman senator was brother of Tiberius Gracchus. On the murder of his brother he left the forum and lived in retirement; but after a time he was elected to office, and accepted it. He soon became a leading tribune.

Among the laws which he procured to increase the authority of the people, and lessen that of the senate, one related to colonizing and dividing the public lands among the poor. Another was in favor of the army, who were now to be clothed at the public charge, without diminution of their pay, and none was to serve till he was full seventeen years old. A third was for the benefit of the Italian allies, who were to have the same right of voting at elections as the citizens of Rome. By a fourth the markets were regulated, and the poor enabled to buy bread-corn at a cheaper rate. A fifth related to the courts of judicature, and, indeed, contributed more than anything to retrench the power of the senate. Before this, senators only were judges in all causes, and on that account their body was formidable both to the equestrian order and to the people. But now he added three hundred knights to the three hundred senators, and decreed that a judicial authority should be equally invested in the six hundred.

The work that he took most pains with was that of the public roads, in which he paid a regard to beauty as well as use. They were drawn in a straight line through the country, and either paved with hewn stone, or made of a binding sand. When he met with dells or other deep holes, he either filled them up with rubbish, or laid bridges over them; so that being leveled and brought to a perfect parallel on both sides, they afforded a regular and elegant prospect through the whole.

Besides, he divided all the roads into miles of near eight furlongs each, and set up pillars of stone to mark the divisions. He likewise erected other stones, at proper distances, on each side of the way, to assist travellers who rode without servants to mount their horses.

But sedition again began to show itself, and Caius quarreled with his colleagues. The reason was this:—There was a show of gladiators to be exhibited to the people in the forum, and most of the magistrates had caused scaffolds to be erected around the place, in order to let them out for hire. Caius insisted that they should be taken down, that the poor might see the exhibition without paying for it. As none of the proprietors regarded his orders, he waited till the night preceding the show, and then went with his own workmen and demolished the scaffolds. Next day the populace saw the place quite clear of them, and, of course, they admired him as a man of superior spirit. But his colleagues were greatly offended at his violent temper and measures, and it was not long before there was an open rupture, and Caius was obliged to flee from Rome. He was pursued, captured, and immediately killed. We are told also that after a person had cut off the head of Caius, and was bearing away the prize, Septimuleius, one of Opimius' friends, took it from him; for the weight in gold had been offered by proclamation for the head. Septimuleius carried it to Opimius upon the point of a pike; and when put into the scales it was found to weigh seventeen pounds eight ounces; but Septimuleius had added fraud to his other villainies, and had taken out the brain and filled the cavity with molten lead.

DEMOSTHENES.

Note.—DEMOSTHENES (Greek). The career of this matchless orator is fully told by Plutarch. He was born near Athens, B.C. 383, and poisoned himself in the temple of Poseidon B.C. 322.

THIS prince of orators was son of Demosthenes, a sword-cutler, one of the principal citizens of Athens. He was only seven years old when his father died, and his guardians greatly neglected him, and squandered or wasted the money which had been left to support and educate him.

His ambition to speak in public is said to have taken its rise on this occasion:—The orator Callistratus was to plead a celebrated cause, and the expectation of the public was greatly raised, both by the powers of the orator—which were then in the highest repute—and by the importance of the trial. Demosthenes, hearing his governors and tutors agree among themselves to attend the trial, prevailed on his master to take him to hear the pleadings. The master, having some acquaintance with the officers who opened the court, got his young pupil a seat where he could hear the orators without being seen. Callistratus had great success, and his abilities were extremely admired. Demosthenes was fired with a spirit of emulation. When he saw with what distinction the orator was conducted home, and complimented by the people, he was struck still more with the power of that commanding eloquence which could carry all before it. From this time, therefore, he bade adieu to the other studies and exercises in which boys are engaged, and applied himself with great assiduity to declaiming, in hopes of being one day numbered among the orators.

When he had attained his majority he called his guardians to account at law, and he wrote orations against them; and as they found many methods for causing delay, he had plenty of opportunities for exercising his talent as an orator at the bar. At first he was laughed at and interrupted, for his violence of manner and his stammering made it very difficult to understand him. He overcame these difficulties by retiring to the country, where he practiced and studied every day both action and speech; and to insure his not going into the city, he shaved off the hair on one side of his head, which compelled him to keep in retirement till it had grown again. Feeling confidence in his oratorical powers, he returned to the bar, and soon began to be listened to and admired. He was seldom heard to speak anything extempore; and though the people often called upon him by name, as he sat in the assembly, to speak to the point debated, he would not do it unless he came prepared. For this many of the orators ridiculed him; and Pytheas, in particular, told him "that all his arguments smelled of the lamp." He did not pretend to deny his previous preparation, but told the orators "that he neither wrote the whole of his orations, nor spoke without first committing part to writing." He further affirmed "that this showed him a good member of a democratic state; for the coming prepared to the rostrum was a mark of respect for the people."

As for his personal defects, Demetrius, the Phalerean, gives us an account of the remedies he applied to them; and he says he had it from Demosthenes in his old age. The hesitation and stammering of his tongue he corrected by practicing to speak with pebbles in his mouth; and strengthened his voice by running or walking up hill, and pronouncing some passage in an oration or a poem during the difficulty of breathing. He had, moreover, a looking-glass in his house, before which he used to declaim, and adjust all his motions.

When Harpalus fled from Alexander (who was in Asia) to Athens, laden with very valuable treasures, he asked the Athenians to give him shelter. Most of the orators had an eye on the gold; but Demosthenes advised that Harpalus should be sent off, as his presence in Athens might provoke war. Yet a few days after, when they were looking over the treasures, Harpalus noticed that Demosthenes seemed particularly pleased with one of the king's cups, and stood admiring the workmanship and fashion. He desired him to take it in his hand, and feel the weight of the gold. Demosthenes being surprised at the weight, and asking Harpalus how much it might bring, he smiled, and said, "It will bring you twenty talents;" and as soon as it was night he sent him the cup with that sum. Harpalus knew well enough how to distinguish a man's passion for gold by his pleasure at the sight, and the keen looks he cast upon it. Demosthenes could not resist the temptation: it made all the impression upon him that was expected; he received the money, and went over to the interest of Harpalus. Next day he came into the assembly with a quantity of wool and bandages about his neck; and when the people called upon him to get up and speak, he made signs that he had lost his voice. Upon this, some that were by said, "It was no common hoarseness he had got in the night; it was a hoarseness occasioned by swallowing gold and silver." Afterward, when all the people were apprised of his taking the bribe, and he wanted to speak in his own defense, they would not suffer him, but raised a clamor, and expressed their indignation. At the same time, somebody or other stood up, and said sneeringly, "Will you not listen to the man with the cup?"

At the same time, Demosthenes, seemingly with a design to prove his innocence, moved for an order that the affair should be brought before the court of Areopagus, and all persons punished who should be found guilty of taking bribes. In consequence of which he appeared before that court, and was convicted, and sentenced to pay a fine of fifty talents, and to be imprisoned till it was paid. The disgrace of his conviction, and the weakness of his constitution—which could not bear close confinement—determined him to fly; and this he did. He bore his exile in a very weak and effeminate manner. He was after a time recalled, and the fine paid for him; but he did not long enjoy the return to his country. He lost his life in the following manner:—When news was brought that Antipater and Craterus were coming to Athens, Demosthenes and his party hastened to escape, and the people immediately condemned them to death. As they fled different ways, Antipater sent a company of soldiers, under Archias, the exile hunter, to pursue and capture them.

Archias being informed that Demosthenes had taken sanctuary in the temple of Neptune at Calauria, he and his Thracian soldiers passed over into it in rowboats. As soon as he was landed he went to the orator, and endeavored to persuade him to quit the temple, and go with him to Antipater, assuring him that he had no hard measure to expect. On hearing which, Demosthenes retired into the inner part of the temple; and taking some paper, as if he meant to write, he put the pen in his mouth, and bit it a considerable time, as he used to do when thoughtful about his composition. He sucked the poison from his pen, after which, he covered his head, fell by the altar, and expired. He died on the 16th of October, B.C. 322, aged 61, leaving behind him a great body of orations.

CICERO.

Note.—CICERO (Roman). Cicero was born B.C. 106, the same year of Pompey's birth, and died B.C. 43.

I THINK the first of the family who bore the name of Cicero must have been an extraordinary man; and for that reason his posterity did not reject the appellation, but rather took to it with pleasure, though it was a common subject of ridicule; for the Latins called a vetch "Cicer," and he had a flat excrescence on the tip of his nose in resemblance of a vetch, from which he got that surname. As for the Cicero of whom we are writing, his friends advised him, on his first application to business, and soliciting one of the great offices of state, to lay aside or change that name. But he answered with great spirit, "That he would endeavor to make the name of Cicero more glorious than that of the Scauri and the Catuli." When quæstor in Sicily, he consecrated in one of the temples a vase, or some other offering, in silver, upon which he inscribed his first two names, Marcus Tullius, and, punning upon the third, ordered the artificer to engrave a vetch. Such is the account we have of his name. As he was naturally ambitious of honor, and being spurred on besides by his father and his friends, he betook himself to the bar. Nor was it by slow and insensible degrees that he gained the palm of eloquence; his fame shot forth at once, and he was distinguished above all the orators of Rome.

His excellence at hitting off a jest or repartee animated his pleadings, and therefore seemed not foreign to the business of the forum; but by bringing it much into use he offended numbers of people, and got the character of a malevolent man. As to his domestic life, we read that he had a handsome country-seat at Arphinum, a farm near Naples, and another at Pompeii, but neither of them was very considerable. His wife Terentia brought him a fortune of a hundred and twenty thousand denarii, and he fell heir to about ninety thousand more. Upon this he lived in a genteel, and at the same time a frugal manner, with men of letters about him, both Greeks and Romans. He rarely took his meal before sunset; not that business or study prevented his sitting down to table sooner, but the weakness of his stomach, he thought, required that regimen. Indeed, he was so exact in all respects in the care of his health, that he had his stated hours for rubbing and for the exercise of walking. By this management of his constitution, he gained a sufficient stock of health and strength for the great labors and fatigues he afterward underwent. He gave up to his brother the town-house which belonged to his family, and took up his residence on the Palatine Hill, that those who came to pay their court to him might not have far to go, and he had a levee every day.

The first great danger which Cicero had to guard against was the conspiracy of Catiline, who, with Lentulus and others, resolved to kill the whole senate, and as many other citizens as they possibly could; to burn the city; and to spare none but the sons of Pompey, who were to be kept as pledges of peace with that general. The conspirators had fixed on a night during the feast of the Saturnalia for the execution of their enterprise. They had lodged arms and combustible matter in the house of Cethegus. They had divided Rome into a hundred parts, and selected the same number of men, each of whom was allotted his quarter to set fire to. As this was to be done by them all at the same moment, they hoped that the conflagration would be general; others were to intercept the water, and kill all that went to seek it.

Cicero discovered the conspiracy in time, and caught Catiline and the rest of the leading conspirators, who were put to death privately. As Cicero passed through the forum to go to his own house, the people hailed him with loud acclamations, and called him "the savior and second founder of Rome." At night the streets were illuminated with a multitude of lamps and torches placed near the doors. The women held out lights from the tops of the houses, that they might behold and pay a proper compliment to the man who was now followed with solemnity by a train of the greatest men in Rome, most of whom had distinguished themselves by successful wars, led up triumphs, and enlarged the empire both by sea and land. All these, in their discourse with each other as they went along, acknowledged that

Rome was indebted to many generals and great men of that age for pecuniary acquisitions, for rich spoils, for power, but for preservation and safety to Cicero alone, who had rescued her from so great and dreadful a danger. Not that his quashing the enterprise and punishing the delinquents appeared so extraordinary a thing; but the wonder was that he could suppress the greatest conspiracy that ever existed with so little inconvenience to the state, and without tumult.

Though he had an insatiable desire for gaining honor, he was never unwilling that others should have their share, for he was entirely free from envy; and it appears from his works that he was most liberal in his praises, not only of the ancients, but of those of his own time. Many of his remarkable sayings, too, of this nature are preserved. Thus, of Aristotle he said, "That he was a river of flowing gold;" and of Plato's dialogues, "That if Jupiter were to speak he would speak as Plato did." Theophrastus used to be his "particular favorite;" and being asked which of Demosthenes' orations he thought the best, he answered, "The longest." Some who affect to be zealous admirers of that orator complain, indeed, of Cicero's saying in one of his epistles, "that Demosthenes sometimes nodded in his orations;" but they forget the many great encomiums he bestowed on him in the other parts of his works; and do not consider that he gave the title of *Philippics* to his orations against Mark Antony, which were the most elaborate he ever wrote. There was not one of his contemporaries, celebrated either for his eloquence or philosophy, whose fame he did not promote either by speaking or writing of him in an advantageous manner.

Cicero's enemies were at last numerous enough to get him banished. The people, however, paid no regard to the decree, but gave him succor and protection. His villas and his house in Rome were burned, and Clodius put his goods up to auction, and the crier gave notice of it every day, but no buyer appeared.

Cicero was recalled sixteen months after his banishment; and such joy was expressed by the cities, so much eagerness to meet him shown by all ranks of people, that his own account of it is less than the truth, though he said "that Italy had brought him on her shoulders to Rome."

He soon regained his popularity, and daily entertained at his own charge persons of honor and learning, not with magnificence indeed, but with elegance and propriety. He had no porter at his gate, nor did any man ever find him in bed; for he rose early in the morning, and kindly received those who came to pay their court to him, either standing or walking before his door. We are told that he never caused any man to be beaten with rods, or to have his garments rent; never uttered opprobrious language in his anger, nor added insult to punishment.

After the battle of Pharsalia between Cæsar and Pompey, and after the flight of Pompey, Cato desired Cicero to take command of part of the fleet, but he declined to have any further share in the war. Upon which young Pompey and his friends called him traitor, drew their swords, and would certainly have dispatched him had not Cato interposed and conveyed him out of the camp. He then withdrew from public business, and bestowed his leisure on the young men who were desirous to be instructed in philosophy. Cicero had no share in the conspiracy against Cæsar, though he was a particular friend of Brutus. Another conspiracy ended in the proscription of Cicero, and he fled by ship to Cajeta, where he had a delightful summer retreat. There was a temple of Apollo on that coast, from which it was observed that a flight of crows came with a great noise, and perched on the sails of Cicero's ship. All looked upon this as an ill omen; yet Cicero went on shore, and, entering his house, lay down to repose himself. In the meantime, a number of the crows settled in the chamber window, and croaked in the most doleful manner. One of them even entered it, and, alighting on the bed, attempted with its beak to draw off the clothes with which he had covered his face. At sight of this, the servants began to reproach themselves. "Shall we," said they, "remain to be spectators of our master's murder? Shall we not protect him, so innocent and so great a sufferer as he is, when the brute creatures give him marks of their care and attention?" Then partly by entreaty, partly by force, they got him into his litter, and carried him toward the sea.

Meantime the assassins came up, and Cicero fell in the sixty-fourth year of his age.

DEMETRIUS.

Note.—DEMETRIUS (Macedonian). Demetrius was born B.C. 338, and, at the age of twenty-two, commanded the army sent against Ptolemy, by whom he was defeated near Gaza.

DEMETRIUS, though tall, was not equal in height to his father, Antigonus. But his beauty and his mien were so inimitable that no sculptor or painter could hit off a likeness. His countenance had a mixture of grace and dignity, and was at once amiable and awful; and the unsubdued and eager air of youth was blended with the majesty of the hero and the king. There was the same happy mixture in his behavior, which inspired, at the same time, both pleasure and awe. In his hours of leisure, he was a most agreeable companion; at his table, and every species of entertainment, of all princes he was the most delicate; and yet, when business called, nothing could equal his activity, his diligence, and dispatch; in which respect he imitated Bacchus most of all the gods, since he was not only terrible in war, but knew how to terminate war with peace, and turn with the happiest address to the joys and pleasures which peace inspires. His affection for his father was remarkably great; and in the respect he paid his mother, his love for his other parent was very discernible.

His war with the Rhodians was occasioned by their alliance with Ptolemy; and in the course of it he brought the largest of his helepoles up to their walls. Its base was square: each of its sides at the bottom forty-eight cubits wide, and it was sixty-six cubits high. The sides of the several divisions gradually lessened, so that the top was much narrower than the bottom. The inside was divided into several stories or rooms, one above another. The front, which was turned toward the enemy, had a window in each storey, through which missive weapons of various kinds were thrown; for it was filled with men who practiced every method of fighting. It neither shook nor veered the least in its motion, but rolled on in a steady upright position, and moved with a horrible noise. He had two coats of mail brought from Cyprus for his use in this war, each of which weighed forty minæ. Zolius, the maker, to show the excellence of their temper, ordered a dart to be shot at one of them from an engine at the distance of twenty-six paces, and it stood so firm that there was no more mark upon it than what might be made with a writing-stylus.

People have remarked that Demetrius always appeared like a theatrical king. He not only affected a superfluity of ornament in wearing a double diadem, and a robe of purple interwoven with gold, but he had his shoes made of a cloth of gold, with soles of fine purple. There was a robe a long time in weaving for him, of most sumptuous magnificence. The figure of the world and all the heavenly bodies were to be represented upon it; but it was left unfinished on account of his change of fortune. Nor did any of his successors ever presume to wear it, though Macedon had many pompous kings after him. This ostentation of dress offended a people who were unaccustomed to such sights; but his luxurious and dissolute manner of life was a more obnoxious circumstance; and what disobliged them most of all was his difficulty of access; for he either refused to see those who applied to him, or behaved to them in a harsh and haughty manner.

One day, when he seemed to come out in a more obliging temper, and to be more accessible, he was presented with several petitions, all which he received, and put them in the skirt of his robe. The people of course followed him with great joy; but no sooner was he come to the bridge over the Axius than he opened his robe and shook all the petitions into the river. This stung the Macedonians to the heart; when, looking for the protection of a king, they found the insolence of a tyrant. An old woman was one day very troublesome to him in the street, and begged with great importunity to be heard. He said, "He was not at leisure." "Then," cried the old woman, "you should not be a king." The king was struck with these words; and having considered a moment, he returned to his palace, where, postponing all other affairs, he gave audience for several days to all who chose to apply to him, beginning with the old woman.

In a battle with his son-in-law, Seleucus, he was abandoned by his soldiers, captured, and, after three years' confinement, he died of a distemper occasioned by idleness and excess. This happened B.C. 284, when he was fifty-four years of age.

ANTONY.

Note.—ANTONY (Roman). Antony the triumvir was born about B.C. 83. The full story of his remarkable career and his death, with that of Cleopatra, are given by Plutarch.

MARK ANTONY had a noble dignity of countenance, a graceful length of beard, a large forehead, an aquiline nose; and, upon the whole, the same manly aspect that we see in the pictures and statues of Hercules. There was, indeed, an ancient tradition that his family was descended from Hercules, and it was no wonder if Antony sought to confirm this opinion by affecting to resemble him in his air and his dress. Thus, when he appeared in public, he wore his vest girt on the hips, a large sword, and over all a mantle. His liberality to the soldiers and to his friends was the first foundation of his advancement, and continued to support him in that power which he was otherwise weakening by a thousand irregularities.

In the conspiracy against Cæsar it was proposed that Antony too should be killed, but Brutus effectually opposed the suggestion. Antony did not know of the plot against Cæsar, and was much concerned when he heard of the assassination. When Cæsar was slain, Antony absconded in the disguise of a slave; but after he found that the conspirators were assembled in the capitol, and had no further designs of massacre, he assembled the senate, when he proposed that an act of amnesty should be passed; and when Cæsar's body was exposed in the forum he undertook the customary funeral oration; and when he found the people affected with his encomiums on the deceased, he endeavored still more to excite their compassion by all that was pitiable or aggravating in the massacre.

Antony fought the enemies of Cæsar with some success, but was in the end defeated and had to fly. He was in terrible straits when he set out in his expedition against the Parthians, and he sent for Cleopatra to answer some charges which had been laid against her of assisting his enemies in the war. Prepared, therefore, with such treasures, ornaments, and presents, as were suitable to the dignity and affluence of her kingdom, but chiefly relying on her personal charms, she set off for Cilicia, to meet Antony.

She sailed along the river Cydnus in a most magnificent galley. The stern was covered with gold, the sails were of purple, and the oars were silver. These, in their motion, kept time to the music of flutes and pipes and harps. The queen, in the dress and character of Venus, lay under a canopy embroidered with gold of the most exquisite workmanship; while boys, like painted Cupids, stood fanning her on each side of the couch. Her maids were of the most distinguished beauty, and, habited like the Nereids and the

Graces, assisted in the steering and conduct of the vessel. The fragrance of burning incense was diffused along the shores, which were covered with multitudes of people. Some followed the procession, and numbers went down from the city to see it. Antony sent to invite her to supper; but she thought it his duty to wait upon her; so, to show his politeness, on her arrival he complied. He was astonished at the magnificence of the preparations, but particularly at the multitude of lights, which were raised or let down together, and disposed in such a variety of square and circular figures that they afforded one of the most pleasing spectacles that has been recorded in history. The day following Antony invited her to sup with him, and was ambitious to outdo her in the elegance and magnificence of the entertainment. But he was soon convinced that he came short of her in both, and was the first to ridicule the meanness and vulgarity of the feast. Notable was the variety of her powers in conversation; her beauty, however, was neither astonishing nor inimitable, but it derived a force from her wit and her fascinating manner, which was absolutely irresistible. Her voice was delightfully melodious, and had the same variety of modulation as a instrument of many strings. She spoke most languages, and there were but few of the foreign ambassadors whom she answered by an interpreter.

To mention all Antony's follies would be too trifling; but his fishing story must not be omitted. He was a-fishing one day with Cleopatra, and had ill success, which in her presence he could but look upon as a disgrace; and he therefore ordered one of the assistants to dive, and put on his hook fish which had been taken before. This scheme he put in practice three or four times, and Cleopatra perceived it. She affected, however, to be surprised at his success, expressed her wonder to the people about her, and the day following invited them to see fresh proofs of it. When the day following came, the vessel was crowded with people; and as soon as Antony had let down his line she ordered one of her divers immediately to put a salt fish on his hook. When Antony found he had caught his fish, he drew up his line; and this, as may be supposed, occasioned no small mirth amongst the spectators. "Go, general!" said Cleopatra, "leave fishing to us petty princes of Pharus and Canopus; your game is cities, kingdoms, and provinces."

After the battle of Actium, where Antony was defeated, it was reported that Cleopatra had killed herself, and Antony immediately determined to follow her example. He plunged his sword into his body, and threw himself on a couch. The wound, however, was not so deep as to cause immediate death. His friends all fled, and left him to his cries and torments, till Diomedes, secretary to Cleopatra, came with her request that he would come to her in the monument. When Antony found that she was still living, it gave him fresh spirits, and he ordered his servants to carry him in their arms to the door of the monument. Cleopatra would not suffer the door to be opened, but a rope being let down from a window, Antony was fastened to it, and she, with her two women (all that were admitted into the monument), drew him up. Nothing could possibly be more affecting than that spectacle. Antony soon after expired, and the death of Cleopatra followed.

It is related by some than an asp was brought in among some figs, and hid under the leaves, and that Cleopatra had arranged so that she might be bitten without seeing it. It is affirmed that she had two small punctures on her arm, apparently occasioned by the sting of the asp; and it is clear that Cæsar gave credit to this, for her effigy, which he carried in triumph, had an asp on the arm; and though Cæsar was much disappointed at her death, he admired her fortitude, and ordered her to be buried in the tomb of Antony, with all the magnificence due to her quality. She died at the age of thirty--nine, after having reigned twenty-two years, the last fourteen in conjunction with Antony. Antony was fifty-three, some say fifty-six, years old when he died.

DION.

Note.—DION (Syracusan). Dion was born B.C. 408 and his death took place fifty-five years later.

AMONGST the many pupils of the famous philosopher Plato, Dion was one of the most distinguished. To the fertility of his genius, and the excellence of his disposition, Plato himself has given testimony, and he did the greatest honor to that testimony in his life. For though he had been educated in servile principles under the tyrant Dionysius,—though he had been familiarized to dependence, on the one hand, and to the indulgence of pomp and luxury, as the greatest happiness, on the other,—yet he was no sooner acquainted with that philosophy which points out the road to virtue, than his whole soul caught the enthusiasm, and, with the simplicity of a young man who judges of the dispositions of others. by his own, he concluded that Plato's lectures would have the same effect on Dionysius. For this reason he solicited, and at length persuaded, the tyrant to hear him. When Plato was admitted, the discourse turned on virtue in general. Afterward they came to fortitude in particular; and Plato made it appear that tyrants have of all men the least pretence to that virtue. Justice was the next topic; and when Plato asserted the happiness of the just, and the wretched condition of the unjust, the tyrant was stung; and being unable to answer his arguments, he expressed his resentment against those who seemed to listen to him with pleasure. At last he was extremely exasperated, and asked the philosopher what business he had in Sicily? Plato answered, "That he came to seek an honest man." "And so, then," replied the tyrant, "it seems you have lost your labor." It was not long before the tyrant turned his hate against Dion, and accused him of conspiring against him, and he banished him.

Dionysius now removed Plato into the citadel, under color of kindness; but in reality to set a guard upon him, lest he should follow Dion, and proclaim to the world how injuriously he had been treated. But in the course of time Plato managed to gain the favor of the tyrant, and was admitted into his presence without the usual formality of being searched. This form had to be gone through by every one, even by his wife and children, before they were admitted to his presence, for fear that they should have weapons or poison about them. The king would not even trust himself to the barber, but burned off his beard with a live coal.

Dion was at length able to march at the head of a formidable army, against Dionysius. He reached Syracuse almost without opposition, and the principal inhabitants, clad in white, met him at the gates and greeted him as their deliverer. The populace fell with great fury on Dionysius' party, but in particular they seized his spies, a set of wretches hated by gods and men, who went about the city to collect the sentiments of the inhabitants in order to communicate them to the tyrant.

Dion had a friend named Calippus, an Athenian, with whom he first became acquainted, not on account of his literary merit, but, according to Plato, because he happened to be introduced by him to some religious mysteries. He had always attended him in the army, and was in great esteem. He was, as before mentioned, the first of his friends who marched along with him into

Syracuse, and he had distinguished himself in every action. This man, finding that Dion's chief friends had fallen in the war, that since the death of Heraclides the popular party was without a leader, and that he himself stood in great favor with the army, formed an execrable design against the life of his benefactor, which was successful.

Dion was fifty years old when he was assassinated.

MARCUS BRUTUS.

Note.—MARCUS BRUTUS (Roman). The mother of Marcus Brutus was a sister of Cato. As stated in the following sketch of his career, his death occurred B.C. 42, when he was in his forty-third year.

BRUTUS had all the advantages that arise from the cultivation of philosophy. To his spirit, which was naturally sedate and mild, he gave vigor and activity by constant application. Upon the whole, he was happily formed to virtue, both by nature and education. Even the partisans of Cæsar ascribe to him everything that had the appearance of honor or generosity in the conspiracy, and all that was of a contrary character they laid to the charge of Cassius, who was, indeed, the friend and relation of Brutus, but by no means resembled him in the simplicity of his manners.

The popularity of the conspiracy against Cæsar made Brutus feel that the safety of some of the greatest men in Rome depended on his conduct, and he could not think of the danger they were to encounter without anxiety. When the day fixed for the assassination came, Brutus went out, and took with him a dagger, which last circumstance was known only to his wife. The rest of the conspirators met at the house of Cassius, and conducted his son, who was that day to put on the toga virilis, to the forum; from whence they proceeded to Pompey's portico, and waited for Cæsar. Though the day was far spent, still Cæsar did not come, being detained by his wife and the soothsayers.

The senate was already seated, and the conspirators soon got close about Cæsar's chair, under pretense of preferring a suit to him. Cassius turned his face to Pompey's statue, and invoked it, as if it had been sensible of his prayers. Trebonius kept Antony in conversation outside the court. And now Cæsar entered, and the whole senate rose to salute him. The conspirators crowded around him, and sent Tullius Cimber, one of their number, to solicit the recall of his brother, who was banished. They all united in the solicitation, took hold of Cæsar's hand, and kissed his head and his breast. He rejected their applications, and, finding that they would not desist, at length rose from his seat in anger. Tullius, upon this, laid hold of his robe, and pulled it from his shoulders. Casca, who stood behind, gave him the first, though but a slight wound, with his dagger near the shoulder. Cæsar caught the handle of the dagger, and said, "Villain! Casca! What dost thou mean?" Cæsar was wounded by numbers almost at the same instant, and looked round him for some way to escape; but when he saw the dagger of Brutus pointed against him, he let go Casca's hand, and, covering his head with his robe, resigned himself to their swords. The conspirators pressed so eagerly to stab him that they wounded each other. Brutus, in attempting to have his share in the sacrifice, received a wound in his hand, and all of them were covered with blood.

Early next morning the senate assembled again, and voted thanks to Antony for preventing a civil war, as well as to Brutus and his party for their services to the commonwealth.

At the battle of Philippi Brutus was defeated by the young Cæsar, and being unable to bear the ignominy, he killed himself, B.C. 42.

ARTAXERXES.

Note.—ARTAXERXES (Persian). Artaxerxes was the third son of Xerxes. He murdered his brother Darius and ascended the throne of Persia B.C. 465. He died B.C. 424 and was succeeded by Xerxes. It is generally believed that Artaxerxes was the Ahasueras of Scripture, who married Esther. Artaxerxes, surnamed Mnemon, the eldest son of Darius, began his reign in B.C. 404 and ruled for forty-two years.

ARTAXERXES THE FIRST, who of all the Persian kings was the most distinguished for his moderation and greatness of mind, was surnamed Longimanus, because his right hand was longer than his left. He was the son of Xerxes. The second

Artaxerxes, of whom we now write, was surnamed Mnemon, because of his wonderful memory. Soon after the death of Darius, the king, his successor, went to Pasargadæ, in order to be consecrated, according to custom, by the priests of Persia. In that city there is the temple of a goddess who has the affairs of war under her patronage, and, therefore, may be supposed to be Minerva. The prince to be consecrated must enter that temple, put off his own robe there, and take that which was worn by the great Cyrus before he was king. He must eat a cake of figs, chew some turpentine, and drink a cup of acidulated milk. Whether there are any other ceremonies is unknown, except to the persons concerned.

One of the chief military exploits during this reign was the great battle of Cunaxa, in which Cyrus, the king's brother, was defeated and slain.

The horrid punishment of "The Boat" is thus described by Plutarch:—They take two boats, which are made to fit on each other, and extend the criminal in one of them in a supine posture. Then they turn the other boat upon it, so that the poor wretch's body is covered, and only the head and hands are out at one end, and the feet at the other. They give him victuals daily, and if he refuses to eat, they compel him by pricking him in the eyes. After he has eaten, they make him drink a mixture of honey and milk, which they pour into his mouth. They spread the same, too, over his face, and always turn him so as to have the sun full in his eyes; the consequence of which is, that his face is covered with swarms of flies. The poor victim is thus left to die a lingering death. The unfortunate victim in this case was named Mithridates, and he found death in seventeen days.

Artaxerxes died a natural death at the age of ninety-four years.

ARATUS.

Note.—ARATUS (Greek). This Greek poet and astronomer was born in Cilicia and flourished about B.C. 300.

WHEN only seven years old Aratus escaped assassination. He was educated by the friends of his family at Argos in a liberal manner, and as he was vigorous and robust he took to gymnastic exercises and gained many prizes. Indeed, in his statues there is an athletic look. Hence, perhaps, it was that he cultivated his powers of eloquence less than became a statesman. He might, indeed, be a better speaker than some suppose; and there are those who judge, from his commentaries, that he certainly was so, though they were hastily written, and attempted nothing beyond common language.

After a revolution, the government of Sicyon fell into the hands of Nicoles, and in order to restore the country to liberty Aratus killed him. Aratus was very jealous of tyrannical power, and joined the republic of Sicyon in the Achæan league. He was chosen the first commander of the Achæan armies, and he drove the Macedonians out of Athens and Corinth. He then made war against the Spartans, but was conquered by Cleomenes, their king. He was more successful in his next campaign, and Cleomenes was defeated. Aratus had soon afterward to seek the aid of Philip, King of Macedonia; and he had to repent of the acquaintance, for Philip, dreading the power and influence of Aratus, caused him and his son to be poisoned.

Thus died Aratus at Ægium, at the age of sixty-one, after he had been seventeen times general of the Achæans. That people were desirous of having him buried there, and would have thought it an honor to give him a magnificent funeral, and a monument worthy of his life and character. But the Sicyonians considered it as a misfortune to have him interred anywhere but amongst them, and therefore persuaded the Achæans to leave the disposal of the body entirely to them. As there was an ancient law that had been observed with religious care, against burying any person within their walls, and they were afraid to transgress it on this occasion, they sent to inquire of the priestess of Apollo at Delphi. She returned a favorable answer, which gave great joy to all the Achæans, particularly the people of Sicyon. They changed the day of mourning into a festival, and, adorning themselves with garlands and white robes, brought the corpse with songs and dances from Ægium to Sicyon. There they selected the most conspicuous ground, and interred Aratus as the founder and deliverer of their city.

WEIGHTS AND MEASURES

MENTIONED IN

PLUTARCH'S LIVES.

WEIGHTS.

	lb.	oz.	dwt.	gr.
Mina or pound, Attic,	..	11	7	16 2/7
Talent (sixty minæ), Attic,	56	11	7	17 1/7
Libra or pound, Roman,	..	10	17	13 5/7

MEASURES OF LENGTH.

	Pace.*	ft.	in.
Foot, Roman,	..	0	11 3/5
Cubit, Roman,	..	1	5 2/5
Pace, Roman,	..	4	10
Furlong, Roman,	120	4	4
Mile, Roman,	967	0	0
Cubit, Grecian,	..	1	6 1/8
Furlong, Grecian,	100	4	4 1/5
Mile, Grecian,	805	5	0

MONEY.

	$ ct.
Quadrans,	1/2
As,	3/5
Sestertius,	.04
Sestertium (= 1000 sestertii),	40.00
Denarius,	.15
Obolus, Attic,	.08
Drachma,	.16
Mina (100 drachmæ),	10.00
Talent (60 minæ),	960.00

The Attic talent was equal to about $1,180; the Hebrew, $1,645 to $1,916.

*The English pace is calculated at 5 feet.

A CHRONOLOGICAL TABLE

From Dacier and Other Writers

	B.C.
DEUCALION'S deluge	1511
Minos I., son of Jupiter and Europa	1401
Minos II., grandson of the first	1250
THESEUS.—The expedition of the Argonauts. Theseus attended Jason in it	1228
Troy taken. Demophoon, the son of Theseus, was at the siege	1180
The return of the Heraclidone to Peloponnesus	1101
The first war of the Athenians against Sparta	1068
Codrus, the last king of Athens, sacrifices himself for his country	1068
The Helots subdued by Agis	1055
The Ionic migration	1040
LYCURGUS flourishes	904
THE FIRST OLYMPIAD.	774
ROMULUS.—Rome built	750
The death of Romulus	713
NUMA POMPILIUS.—Numa elected king	712
Numa dies	669
SOLON.—Solon flourishes	598
Cylon's conspiracy	
Epimenides goes to Athens, and expiates the city. He dies soon after, at the age of 154. The seven wise men: Æsop and Anacharsis flourish.	594

	B.C.
Solon Archon	592
Crœsus, king of Lydia	590
Pythagoras goes into Italy	578
Pisistratus sets up his tyranny	570
Cyrus, king of Persia	557
Crœsus taken	547
PUBLICOLA is chosen consul in the room of Collatinus. Brutus fights Aruns, the eldest son of Tarquin. Both are killed	506
Publicola consul the third time. His colleague, Horatius Pulvillus, dedicates the temple of Jupiter Capitolinus	504
Horatius Cocles defends the Sublician bridge against the Tuscans	502
Publicola dies	500
Zeno Eleates flourished	499
The battle of Marathon	489
CORIOLANUS is banished, and retires to the Volsci	488
Herodotus is born	486
Coriolanus besieges Rome; but being prevailed upon by his mother to retire, is stoned to death by the Volsci	485
ARISTIDES is banished for ten years, but recalled at the expiration of three	481
THEMISTOCLES.—The battle of Salamis	478
The battle of Platæa	477
Thucydides is born	474
Themistocles is banished by the Ostracism	469
Artaxerxes ascends the throne of Persia	465
CIMON beats the Persians both at sea and land	460
Socrates is born. He lived 71 years	469
Cimon dies. Alcibiades born the same year. Herodotus and Thucydides flourish; the latter is twelve or thirteen years younger than the former	449
Pindar dies, 80 years old	440
PERICLES stirs up the Peloponnesian war, which lasts 27 years. He was very young when the Romans sent the Decemviri to Athens for Solon's laws	429
Pericles dies	427

	B.C.
Plato born	426
Xerxes killed by Artabanus	424
NICIAS.—The Athenians undertake the Sicilian war	413
Nicias beaten and put to death in Sicily	411
ALCIBIADES takes refuge at Sparta, and afterward amongst the Persians	410
Dionysius the elder, now tyrant of Sicily	409
Sophocles dies, aged 91	407
Euripides dies, aged 75	406
LYSANDER puts an end to the Peloponnesian war, and establishes the thirty tyrants at Athens	403
Thrasybulus expels them	402
Alcibiades put to death by order of Pharnabazus	401
ARTAXERXES MNEMON overthrows his brother Cyrus in a great battle. The retreat of the ten thousand Greeks, conducted by Xenophon	399
Socrates dies	398
AGESILAUS ascends the Spartan throne	395
Lysander sent to the Hellespont	394
Agesilaus defeats the Persian cavalry. Lysander dies	394
The Romans lose the battle of Allia	387
CAMILLUS retires to Ardea	386
Aristotle born	382
Demosthenes born	381
Chabrias defeats the Lacedæmonians	374
Peace between the Athenians and Lacedæmonians	369
The important battle of Leuctra	369
PELOPIDAS, general of the Thebans. He headed the sacred band the year before at Leuctra, where Epaminondas commanded in chief	368
Dionysius the elder, tyrant of Sicily, dies, and is succeeded by his son	366
Isocrates flourishes	364
TIMOLEON kills his brother Timophanes, who was setting himself up as tyrant in Corinth	363
Pelopidas defeats Alexander, the tyrant of Pheræ, but falls in the battle	363

	B.C.
The famous battle of Mantinea, in which Epaminondas, though victorious, is killed by the son of Xenophon..	361
Camillus dies...	360
Artaxerxes dies. So does Agesilaus..................	359
DION expels Dionysius the younger..................	355
Alexander the Great born...............................	353
Dion is killed by Calippus..............................	353
DEMOSTHENES begins to thunder against Philip. Xenophon dies, aged 90...................................	350
Plato dies, aged 80 or 81.................................	346
Timoleon sent to assist the Syracusans..............	335
Dionysius, the younger, sent off to Corinth.........	341
Epicurus born..	339
The battle of Chæronea, in which Philip beats the Athenians and Thebans................................	336
Timoleon dies..	335
ALEXANDER THE GREAT is declared general of all Greece against the Persians, upon the death of his father, Philip...	335
The battle of the Granicus...............................	334
The battle of Arbela.......................................	325
Porus beaten...	326
Diogenes dies, aged 90....................................	324
Alexander dies, aged 33...................................	323
Aristotle dies, aged 63....................................	319
PHOCION retires to Polyperchon, but is delivered up by him to the Athenians, who put him to death..	316
EUMENES, who had attained to a considerable rank amongst the successors of Alexander the Great, is betrayed to Antigonus, and put to death............	314
DEMETRIUS, surnamed Poliocertes, permitted by his father, Antigonus, to command the army in Syria, when only twenty-two years of age..........	312
He restores the Athenians to their liberty, but they choose to remain in the worst of chains, those of servility and meanness	305
Dionysius, the tyrant, dies at Heraclea, aged 55......	303

A CHRONOLOGICAL TABLE.

	B.C.
In the year before Christ 288, died Theophrastus, aged 85............	288
And in the year before Christ 285, Theocritus flourished....	285
PYRRHUS, king of Epirus, passes over into Italy, where he is defeated by Lævinus........	272
The first Punic war, which lasted 24 years........	263
Philopœmen born........	252
ARATUS, of Sicyon, delivered his native city from the tyranny of Nicocles........	249
AGIS and CLEOMENES, contemporaries with Aratus, for Aratus being beaten by Cleomenes, calls in Antigonus from Macedonia, which proves the ruin of Greece........	225
PHILOPŒMEN 30 years old when Cleomenes took Megalopolis. About this time lived Hannibal, Marcellus, Fabius Maximus, and Scipio Africanus......	221
The second Punic war, which lasted 18 years........	217
Hannibal beats the consul Flaminius at the Thrasymenean lake;........	215
And the consuls Varro and Æmilius at Cannæ........	214
He is beaten by Marcellus at Nola........	212
CATO THE CENSOR was 21 or 22 years old when Fabius Maximus took Tarentum. See above......	214
MARCELLUS takes Syracuse........	210
FABIUS MAXIMUS seizes Tarentum........	207
Fabius Maximus dies........	201
Scipio triumphs over his conquests in Africa........	199
TITUS QUINCTIUS FLAMINIUS elected consul at the age of 30	196
All Greece restored to her liberty, by T.Q. Flaminius. Flaminius triumphs; Demetrius, the son of Philip, and Nabis, tyrant of Lacedæmon, follow his chariot.	194
Cato triumphs over his conquests in Spain........	193
Scipio Africanus dies........	182
CÆSAR defeats Pompey at Pharsalia........	46
Cato the younger dies.	
Pompey flies into Egypt, and is assassinated there.	46
Cæsar makes himself master of Alexandria, and sub-	

	B.C.
dues Egypt; after which he marches into Syria, and soon reduces Pharnaces	45
He conquers Juba, Scipio, and Petreius, in Africa, and leads up four triumphs. Previous to which, Cato kills himself	44
Cæsar defeats the sons of Pompey at Munda. Cneius falls in the action, and Sextus flies into Sicily. Cæsar triumphs the fifth time	43
Cicero died in his 64th year	43
BRUTUS.—Cæsar is killed by Brutus and Cassius	42
Brutus passes into Macedonia	41
MARK ANTONY beaten the same year by Augustus at Modena. He retires to Lepidus. The triumvirate of Augustus, Lepidus, and Antony, who divide the empire amongst them.	41
The battle of Philippi, in which Brutus and Cassius, being overthrown by Augustus and Antony, lay violent hands on themselves	40
Antony leagues with Sextus, the son of Pompey, against Augustus	39
Augustus and Antony renew their friendship after the death of Fulvia, and Antony marries Octavia.	38
Augustus and Antony again embroiled	31
The battle of Actium. Antony is beaten, and flies into Egypt with Cleopatra	30
Augustus makes himself master of Alexandria. Antony and Cleopatra destroy themselves	30
Horace dies, aged 57	8

The Christian Era begins.

INDEX.

	PAGE		PAGE
ABANTES	16	Aquarium	115
Absolute monarchy	37	Aratus	222
Achæan league	222	Archidamus	52
Acron	22	Archimedes	79
Actium (battle of)	214	Areopagus . 38, 39,	200
Adrastus	19	Ariadne	16, 17
Ægos Potamos (battle of)	102	Ariamenes	43
		Aristides	42, 84
Æthra	15	Aristotle	156
Agariste	50	Artaxerxes	220
Agesilaus	133	Artemisium (fight at)	43
Agis	185		
Ajax	63	Artillerymen	82
Alcibiades	63, 102	Asp kills Cleopatra	215
Alexander	135, 154	Asparagus	175
Allia (river)	48	Attica	17
Amazons	18	Aventine, Mount	21
Ambrones	100		
Aminias	44	BATH, grooms of	165
Anaxagoras	51	Battery (naval)	79
Anaximenes	41	Battle signal	147
Anio (river)	50	Beards cut off	16
Antigonus	132, 190	Bees	40
Antiope	18	Belgæ	141
Antium	58	Black days	112
Antony (Mark)	205, 211	Bloody corn	58
Apollo	223	Boat (punish't)	221
Apollonius	172	Bœotia	78
Apothetæ	28	Boroughs	34

INDEX.

	PAGE		PAGE
Boundaries	18	Cleomenes	188
Brennus	48	Cleopatra	161, 179, 212
Bribery	69, 200	Cleophylus	25
Britain	175	Clinias	63
Britons	141	Clothing	182
Brundusium	146	Coalemos (idiot)	108
Brutus (Marcus)	218	Coat of mail	209
Bucephalus	155, 164, 167	Coinage	26
Building ruination	123	Cold wine	170
Bull's blood	45, 92	Company halls	34
Burials	31, 134, 223	Coriolanus	67
		Corpses	31
Cæcias	128	Corynetes	18
Cæsar, Julius	171, 219	Country life	34
Caius Marius	98	Court hall	18
Calendar	35, 181	Crassus (Marcus)	123
Calippus	217	Cretan frugality	25
Camillus	45	Crimesus (river)	71
Candidates	69	Critias	66
Casca	181, 219	Crommyonian Sow	15
Cassius	219	Cross and snake	191
Catiline	203	Crows (omen)	207
Cato (Censor)	86	Crucifixion, a	170
Cato	143, 173, 207	Cunaxa (battle of)	221
Cato (the younger)	183	Curius	94
Celer	21	Cyprus	209
Celeres	24, 32	Cyprus (Soli)	40
Celibacy	105	Cyrus	169
Centaurs	19	Cyrus (the younger)	102
Ceres	66		
Chance	72	Damon	51
Characitani	127	Darius	157
Chariot (triumph)	47	Dead men	38
Chickens	192	Dead soldiers	119
Chief priest	32	Debt-cutters	38
Cicero	172, 202	Debtors	118
Cimon	20, 42, 108	Delos	17
Citium (siege of)	109	Delphi	16, 17
Citizens' supper	108	Delphinian Apollo	16

INDEX.

	PAGE		PAGE
Demetrius	208	Faustulus	21
Democracy	25	Favonius	145
Demosthenes, 120, 157,	197	Fences abolished	104
Dice	64, 185	Fight in a city	96
Diet, spare	28	Fines	133
Diogenes	157	Fire, from sun	33
Diomedes	214	Fires in city	123
Dion	215	Fire stones	58
Dionysius	216	First fruits (hair)	16
Ditches	39	Fishing (Antony)	214
Draco's laws	38	Flaminius, T. Q.	59, 91
Dress of women	39	Flute, the	64
Dust in war	129	Fortune	72
		Fulvius	92
		Funeral orations	39, 212
EARTHQUAKE	59	Funerals	39
Eclipses 55, 120,	163		
Education	27	GAUGAMELA (battle of)	163
Egypt's queen	179	Gauls, at Rome	48
Elephants 83, 95,	167	Geese, the sacred	49
Elephenor	20	Good, Phocion the	183
Eleusis	66	Gracchus, Caius	194
Embalming	140	Gracchus, Tiberius	192
Entertainments	142, 185	Guardians	197
Epaminondas	78	Gylippus	121
Ephori	133, 891	Gymnastics	222
Epirus	93		
Epitaph (Cyrus's)	169		
Euboea	42	HAIR	16, 29
Eumolpidæ	66	Hannibal, 58, 59, 60, 83, 92	
Eumenes	130	Head, weight in gold	196
Euripides	65	Helepoles	209
Execestides	36	Helicon	164
		Hephæstion	171
FABII, THE	56	Herodotus	19
Fabius Maximus	56	High Court	39
Falerians	58	Hippoclus	77
Falling stars	103		
False news	123		

	PAGE		PAGE
Homer	25, 156	Lysander	66, 102
Honest man	216	Lysimachus	84
House expenses	54		
Husbandmen	18	MACEDONIA	78
		Malli, the	168
IDLENESS punished	38	Manlius	92
Illuminations	213	Marathonian bull	16
Intramural burials	223	Marcellus	79
Ion	54	Marcellus (Cæsar)	144
Isthmian games	18	Marcius	32
		Marcus Brutus	218
JANUS (temple of)	36	Marcus Crassus	123
Jason	19	Marius	98
Judicature	195	Mark Antony	205, 211
Juno's temple	46	Markets	195
Just, Aristides the	84	Marseilles	37
Justice	216	Mathematics	82
		Meals	161
LABYRINTH	17	Mechanics (men)	53
Lacedæmon	52	Median war	20
Lamps	204	Meleager	19
Land, division of	25	Menestheus	19
Languages	213	Messenia	78
Laughter, god of	30	Milestones	196
Lawsuits	30	Military tribunes	46
Legion	21	Mines in war	46
Lending money	118, 185	Minotaur	16
Leonidas	161	Minucius	61
Lesche	28	Mithridates	139, 222
Leuctra (battle of)	78, 134	Mithridatic war	33
Libraries	117, 178	Mnemon	221
Lisping	63	Mourning	33
Livy	92	Munda (battle of)	180
Longimanus	220		
Lucullus	109	NAVAL fight	43
Luxury	115	Neoptolemus	94, 131
Lycomedes	19, 44	Nicias	118
Lycurgus	24	Nicon (elephant)	96
Lyre, the	64	Nightingale	29

INDEX. 235

	PAGE		PAGE
Nobleman	18	Pirates	137, 171
Numa	31	Plato 182, 185, 205, 216	
		Poison, death by,	183, 201
OIL-TRADE (Plato's)	37		
Olympias	52	Polymachus	169
Olympic games	42, 65	Polytion	66
Omens	71, 103, 162	Pompey	125, 135
Onion-head	51	Pompey, jun	207
Oratory (bar)	125	Pompey's statue,	181, 219
Ostracism, the	45, 85		
Ox (on money)	18	Pomponius	32
Oxen in war	60	Pontifices, the	33
		Pontifix Maximus	32
PAGI, or boroughs	34	Pontius	48
Palatine Hill	203	Presages	192
Palm (victor's)	17	Prodigies	58
Parsley as an omen	71	Proserpine	66
Patricians	21	Prytaneum	18
Paulus Æmilius	73	Ptolemy	153, 208
Pelopidas	77	Publicola	40, 41
Peloponnesian war,	55, 103	Public tables	26
		Public works	53
Pen, poison in the	201	Publius	142
People's friend	41	Purple robe	209
Pericles	50	Pydna (battle of)	74
Perpenna	130	Pyrrhus	93
Perpetual fire	33		
Perseus	74	QUIRITES	31
Petitions	210	Quoits	27
Phædo	20		
Pharsalia (battle of),	151, 178, 206	REMONIUM	21
		Remus	21
Philip	154, 223	Republic	222
Philippi (battle of)	220	Riot, a	194
Philippics	205	Roads	195
Philochorus	19	Rome rebuilt	50
Philopœmen	90	Rome taken	48
Phocion	182	Romulus	20
Pindar	43	Rubicon	145, 177

INDEX.

	PAGE
SABINE women	22, 23
Sacred lamp	106
Sacrifices	161
Salamis (battle of)	43
Sambuca	81
Sarpedon	184
Schinocephalus	50
Scipio	142
Sciron	15
Secretaries	175
Senate	22, 25
Serpents	191
Sertorius	126
Sight-seeing	196
Sinnis	15
Socrates	65
Solon	36
Soothsayers	219
Sosicles	44
Spain (Cæsar in)	172
Spartan simplicity	186
Speeches (Phocion's)	182
Spies	127, 217
Spleen, cure for	94
Stammering	199
Strangers	124
Superstitions	51, 170
Supper	190
Sylla	101, 105, 135
Syracuse (siege of)	70, 79, 119
TARENTINES, the	94
Teeth (curious)	94
Teleclides	51
Thasymenus (lake)	59
Theatricals	52
Thebes	19

	PAGE
Themistocles	42
Theodorus	66
Theseus	15
Thessalus	66
Thirty tyrants	66
Thrushes	116
Thucydides	52, 57
Tile kills Pyrrhus, a	97
Timoleon	70
Titus Flaminius	91
Toga virilis	219
Tomb of Cyrus	169
Trade companies	34
Trades (various)	53
Treats and gratuities	69
Trebia (battle of)	58
Tree-planting	39
Triumph, a	74
Triumphs	140
Trojan war	20
Trophy, war	22
Truce for burying	19
Turpentine	221
Tuscany	58
Tusculum	86
Tyndaridæ	19
Tyre (siege of)	161
VALERIUS FLACCUS	87
Veii (siege of)	46
Veni, vidi, vici	179
Verrucosus	56
Vest	211
Vestal virgins	33
Vetch	202
Vinegar as a drink	87
Virgins' exercises	27
Votes sold	176

	PAGE		PAGE
WEALTH (Solon's)	37	XANTHIPPUS	50
Widows (soldiers')	46	Xerxes	43, 115
Wills	39		
Wine bath	28	YEAR, days in	35
Wolf (Romulus)	21		
Women (laws)	39	ZAMA (battle of)	92
Women in war	100	Zela (battle of)	179
Wrestlers	27, 64, 90	Zeno	51

COMMON ERRORS
IN
WRITING AND SPEAKING

WHAT THEY ARE AND HOW TO AVOID THEM

WITH A PRACTICAL TREATISE ON
PRONUNCIATION AND PUNCTUATION

By EDWARD S. ELLIS, M.A.

Bound in Cloth Boards, Colored Edges, 50 Cents

WHO does not wish to know how to write and speak the English language correctly? And how few possess that ability! The best educated, even editors and authors, sometimes write sentences that will not bear the test of rhetorical construction or grammatical analysis. The universality of such errors is one of the most astonishing facts connected with our literature.

A second fact, however, is the absolute ease with which a writer or speaker can free himself from a careless and inaccurate style through a careful study of

"COMMON ERRORS IN WRITING AND SPEAKING."

This has been prepared by a scholar noted for the purity and beauty of his style, and the directions are so simple, the explanations so clear, and the suggestions so practical, that the work is worth all the other books on the subject put together.

It is pre-eminently a book for to-day, not for fifty years ago, but one which recognizes our steadily changing modes of expression, the elastic nature of our language, and the evolution that is continually in progress.

FOR SALE AT ALL BOOKSELLERS, OR WILL BE SENT PREPAID ON RECEIPT OF THE PUBLISHED PRICE.

THE WOOLFALL COMPANY
Publishers and Importers

114 Fifth Avenue   NEW YORK

THE YOUTH'S
Classical Dictionary

FOR BOYS AND GIRLS

CONTAINING
BRIEF AND ACCURATE ACCOUNTS OF THE PROPER NAMES
MENTIONED IN CLASSICAL LITERATURE

Edited with Introduction
By EDWARD S. ELLIS, M.A.

Bound in Cloth Boards, Colored Edges, 50 Cents.

THIS work, divested of all coarseness, supplies within the range of a handy volume the labors of Lempriere.

All who would lay claim to scholarship will find this dictionary an absolute necessity. Our modern literature, including even that of the daily press, abounds with classical allusions, the meaning of which is rarely understood by the best educated without referring to a classical dictionary.

Unlike most classical dictionaries, *this* may be taken into the home and read aloud without fear of offending the most sensitive. The youth of tender years may read from it and be instructed in the wisdom of the ancients without fear of contamination. At the same time all that is necessary to a perfect understanding of the subjects is retained; all that is vulgar and harmful to our youth is omitted. The work, therefore, is peculiarly adapted to schools and families, and especially to young students. All who desire to become fully versed in classical literature will find this work indispensable.

FOR SALE AT ALL BOOKSELLERS, OR WILL BE SENT
PREPAID ON RECEIPT OF THE PUBLISHED PRICE.

THE WOOLFALL COMPANY
Publishers and Importers

114 Fifth Avenue   NEW YORK

THE YOUTH'S
Dictionary of Mythology

FOR BOYS AND GIRLS

CONTAINING
BRIEF AND ACCURATE ACCOUNTS OF THE GODS AND GODDESSES OF THE ANCIENTS

Edited with Introduction
By EDWARD S. ELLIS, M.A.

Bound in Cloth Boards, Colored Edges, 50 Cents.

FOLLOWING the plan of the series, this work has been prepared with a view of giving within the limits of a handy volume concise and accurate accounts of the gods and goddesses of the ancients which shall be free from all objectionable matter.

Everywhere, in picture gallery and museum, we are continually reminded of these deities and heroes—these legends and traditions of Pagan nations. They play their part in the poet's thought, are portrayed by the painter's and sculptor's art, and not unfrequently made to serve the purpose of illustration in the literature of to-day. But fully to enjoy and understand these allusions, it is not now necessary for one to wade through a library of volumes, even if such volumes were accessible, since in the "Youth's Dictionary of Mythology" all needful information upon the subject, including the proper pronunciation of the more important mythological names, will be found. This work is not exclusively confined to Roman and Greek mythology, but includes Egyptian, Hindoo and Scandinavian deities and heroes, to which our literature so frequently refers.

FOR SALE AT ALL BOOKSELLERS, OR WILL BE SENT PREPAID ON RECEIPT OF THE PUBLISHED PRICE.

THE WOOLFALL COMPANY
Publishers and Importers

114 Fifth Avenue　　　　　　　　　　　　NEW YORK

www.ingramcontent.com/pod-product-compliance
Lightning Source LLC
Chambersburg PA
CBHW031747230426
43669CB00007B/525